*Surviving the Fall*

# Surviving the Fall

*The Personal Journey of an AIDS Doctor*

Peter A. Selwyn, M.D.

Yale University Press
New Haven & London

Parts of this book appeared in substantially different form in "HIV Therapy in the Real World," *AIDS* 10 (1996): 1591–93; "Caring for HIV-Infected Drug Users: A Provider's Perspective," *Bulletin of the New York Academy of Medicine* 72 (1995): 211–16; and "Before Their Time: A Clinician's Reflections on Death and AIDS," in *Facing Death: Where Culture, Religion, and Medicine Meet,* ed. Howard M. Spiro, Mary G. McCrea Curnen, and Lee Palmer Wandel, 33–37 (New Haven: Yale University Press, 1996).

Designed by Rebecca Gibb.

Set in Fournier type by The Composing Room of Michigan, Inc.

Printed in the United States of America by Vail-Ballou Press, Binghamton, New York.

Library of Congress Cataloging-in-Publication Data

Selwyn, Peter A.
    Surviving the fall : the personal journey of an AIDS doctor / Peter A. Selwyn.
        p.   cm.
    ISBN 0-300-07126-4 (cloth : alk. paper)
    1. Selwyn, Peter A.    2. AIDS (Disease)—New York (State)—Bronx County (N.Y.)    3. Physicians—New York (State)—Bronx County (N.Y.)—Biography.
    I. Title.
RC607.A26S429    1998
616.97′92′0092—dc21
[B]
97-15292

A catalogue record for this book is available from the British Library.

The paper in this book meets the guidelines for permanence and durability of the Committee on Production Guidelines for Book Longevity of the Council on Library Resources.

10  9  8  7  6  5  4  3  2  1

*To my father, who left*
*To my mother, who stayed*
*To my wife, who saw inside me*
*To my daughters, who taught me unconditional love*

Men make their own history, but they do not make it just as they please; they do not make it under circumstances chosen by themselves, but under circumstances directly encountered, given and transmitted from the past.

Karl Marx, *The 18th Brumaire of Louis Bonaparte*, 1869

We all grow up with the weight of history on us. Our ancestors dwell in the attics of our brains as they do in the spiraling chains of knowledge hidden in every cell of our bodies.

Shirley Abbott, *Womenfolk, Growing Up Down South*, 1983

AIDS is kind of like life, just speeded up.

Javon P., heroin addict with AIDS, Bronx, New York, 1988

# Contents

# Foreword

At the end of a long surgical career, I deliberately look back on the particular personal failing for which I feel the most regret. My conscience is not relieved by the near-universality of the shortcoming that is the source of my self-reproach, nor am I forgiven by an awareness that the failing is the virtually inevitable outcome of the biotechnological culture of medicine's past three decades. I know better than to have succumbed, and the existence of mitigating circumstances does not by one whit decrease my culpability.

The fault I so lament is the product of the single greatest problem facing a profession in which compassion, empathy and dedication to a pastoral calling have long been idealized as the traditional hallmarks of commitment to the relief of human suffering, even though they have for the most part been incompletely attained. Medicine's and my great problem and great fault consist of what might be called the intellectualization—the enrapturement with science and technology—by which that legion of men and women who are today's doctors have allowed themselves to become besotted. To be fair, it must be pointed out that this phenomenon has not occurred to the absolute exclusion of our instincts of humanity toward our patients. Still, it has nevertheless indubitably displaced them as the primary motive of care.

I would regret less keenly had I not, along the way, encountered a few physicians whose day-to-day devotion to the individual humanity of their patients has stood out as a veritable beacon, to demonstrate that the wishful role of personal goodness can for an occasional doctor remain the focus of healing. In that gifted—in the sense that their lives are a gift to their patients and to the rest of us—albeit minuscule company, the primacy of steadfast caring is not incompatible with great skill in the use of scientific medicine's most advanced methodologies. The career of Peter Selwyn has been such a luminosity.

In 1992, aware that my expertise in the details of HIV infection was insufficient to write knowledgeably about the disease, I spent some six weeks making rounds and going to conferences with the AIDS team at the Yale–New Haven Medical Center. My aim was to acquaint myself with the atmosphere in which this modern plague presents itself in the hospital environment. It was my good fortune that Peter Selwyn was the attending physician directing the team during most of that time. Since that brief experience, I have often had occasion to describe how taken I was with the dedication of the medical and other personnel who care for people with AIDS, and I have done so in both conversation and print. Much of my image of those devoted physicians comes specifically from having watched Peter Selwyn. For an older, case-hardened observer of the hectic atmosphere that usually pervades a university teaching service, it was enormously impressive to be witness to the quiet, self-assured way in which this sensitive, mature young man addressed the needs of those desperately ill men and women over whom he watched. In my admiring eyes, he became the representation of what a doctor should be.

A few years later, I was immensely pleased to learn that Peter Selwyn had decided to write a book about his clinical experiences. Especially because the great majority of his patients have come from a population too often underserved and misunderstood—those whose disease is in one way or another the result of the destructive combination of poverty, alienation, and drugs—I was certain that his insights would bring a hitherto unexplored dimension to the majority culture's responsiveness. Knowing of no more authoritative medical voice than his, I began eagerly to await the manuscript as soon as I heard that he had completed it. But the pages I finally received contained a treasure far richer than I had anticipated.

My astonishingly perceptive colleague has undertaken no less than a journey back to the beginnings of himself, and then forward again into the present of the man he has become. As he so correctly says early in his book, "Everything in my life led, inexorably, to my arriving at the right place, as a physician in the midst of the AIDS epidemic." He proceeds then to take his reader along on the pilgrimage he has taken to his early childhood, in order to understand the origins of his commitment and the burden he carries with him into the sickroom of each of his patients: "I have learned that the greatest gift I can give to patients is to allow the awareness of my own pain and loss to deepen my solidarity with them, as they stand facing their illness and death." The pain and loss are the unresolved reverberation of his father's suicide when Peter was eighteen months old. As he traces the threads of himself backward to that time—and even to that place—he carries us with him on a circular pathway that emerges finally into the fabric of his adult life. Having been at his side, we come to know why it is that he can be so certain of being now "at the right place." In the full strength of his maturity as a man, Peter Selwyn has stopped to take account of himself, and he now understands, as should each of us, that his past is a piece with his present. He has still a long way to go until completing what will be the voyage of his full life, but the rest of the way will be traveled with the confidence of a man who understands others because he understands himself.

> Sherwin B. Nuland, M.D.
> Clinical professor of surgery
> Yale School of Medicine

# Acknowledgments

This book has been a labor of love, a process of bringing out a story that in some respects was hidden inside me. But it is much more than my own story, and there are many people who helped me in one way or another along the way. I would like to give special thanks to the following:

To my family, for their love, belief, and acceptance.

To all my patients and their families, for their courage, inspiration, and for the privilege of being a witness to their lives, through which I learned so much about my own.

To all my former colleagues on the medical staff of the Montefiore Drug Abuse Treatment Program, and especially Dolores Addo, Janice Colley, Anita Iezza, Meera Satyadeo, Karen Kennedy, Rafael Torres, Monique

Breindel, Anat Feingold, Verna Robertson, Bill Wasserman, Ernie Drucker, Marc Gourevitch, Jane Shaw, John Welton, Vivian Welton, Zach Rosen, Brian Saltzman, Nancy Bermon, Wanda Jiminez, Ardella Adegbo, Jerry Ahern, Valerie Ballard, Iris Parris, Socorro Hamilton, Lyn Mehan, Lea Tenneriello, and Marjorie Nicholson, for the dedication and commitment that made it possible to provide such special care to our patients. In addition, to my colleagues in the Montefiore AIDS Research Program—Jerry Friedland, Bob Klein, Ellie Schoenbaum, Diana Hartel, Katherine Davenny, Susan Tozzi, Irene Fleming, Donna Buono, Phil Alcabes, Marguerite Mayers, Rosemary De Croce, Bob Cicarelli, Ingrid Symes, and Rose Rivera—for your collaboration, partnership, and hard work, which enabled our program to grow from its modest beginnings in a basement office at Montefiore to dimensions we could never have envisioned.

To the many people who have given me valuable advice, feedback, and encouragement concerning this book, in particular Shep Nuland, Ron Taffel, Bernie Siegel, Peter Guzzardi, Richard Morrison, Dan Heaton, Larry Siegel, Vic Sidel, Marc Gourevitch, Jerry Friedland, Jon Ehrlich, Karen Nelson, Stanley Marcus, Ruth Marcus, Connie Peters, Jon Baird, Carl Schwartz, Steve Batki, Renslow Sherer, Al Novick, Ann Williams, and Claire Blatchford, for helping me to believe that this was a project worth pursuing.

To my editor at Yale University Press, Jean Thomson Black, for her receptiveness to this book and for her strong, consistent support throughout the process of publication.

To my senior administrative assistant, Ernestine Jones, for her quiet proficiency, thoroughness, and patience over the past year in working on this manuscript and deciphering my close-to-illegible handwriting.

To Elisabeth Kübler-Ross and all of my friends on the former staff of the Elisabeth Kübler-Ross Center, for helping me to reclaim my history and my life. In particular to Larry Lincoln, Megan Bronson, Jeanette

Philips, Sheila Hill, Connie Toverud, Susa Wuorinen, Alba Payas, Roz Leiser, Lea Abdnor, Frank Monastero, David Mullins, Nancy Mullins, Mark Trommer, Joan Treichler, Jacob Watson, Emmaline Weidman, Adriaan Van Der Hor, Sam Price, Sandy Stewart, Susanna Stewart, Ann Taylor Lincoln, Sharon Tobin, and Cap Easterly, for your love, support, and friendship. It has been an honor and a privilege to know you, to learn from you, and to share with you.

And finally, and in all seriousness, to my cat Scrubby, for staying up with me on many an all-nighter, and to my dog Maya, for her joyful accompaniment with me on long walks in the woods during the fall of 1995—she as a new puppy, I with Dictaphone in hand—as I began the process of remembering and telling the stories which make up this book.

To all of you, I could not have done this without you.

# Introduction

I have become an "AIDS doctor," an outcome I never could have anticipated when I graduated from medical school in 1981. I have been involved
in the care of more than a thousand patients with HIV infection, and for almost ten years these have been my only patients. I have been fundamentally changed by this experience, and my history is now indelibly linked
with the faces and histories of my patients, especially the many hundreds
who have died. This story is their story, and mine.

The beginning of the AIDS epidemic in the Bronx in the early 1980s
was a time without recent precedent, a time when a fatal blood-borne
disease spread, without warning and with grim efficiency through an unsuspecting and vulnerable population. This same insidious pattern was

unfolding in Harlem, Brooklyn, and many other poor, inner-city communities in the United States and around the world. In these communities AIDS was affecting poor, minority populations, primarily intravenous drug users, their sexual partners, and children, in addition to gay men. I have long felt that this history and these stories need to be told, to help honor and take notice of all the uncelebrated men, women, and children who lived and died with this unforgiving plague. Statistics have been described as human beings with the tears washed off. In this narrative, I have tried to restore some humanity to the statistics.

I came to the Bronx from Boston in June 1981 as an intern in family medicine at Montefiore Medical Center. I had just graduated from Harvard Medical School, the same month and year that the first cases of AIDS were reported by the Centers for Disease Control (CDC). I left the Bronx for New Haven in January of 1992, when I was recruited to help direct the AIDS Program at Yale–New Haven Hospital as an associate professor at the Yale School of Medicine. During that decade, AIDS metamorphosed from an unknown entity into the leading cause of death for young adults in New York City and many other urban centers around the world. Those years were also my late twenties and thirties, a time that typically includes the passage from youth to adulthood. During that decade I got married, became a parent, became self-supporting, established my career, and began to have glimpses of my own limitations and mortality that had not been part of my lingering adolescent worldview. This memoir, then, is about not only the coming of age of the epidemic, but also my own.

This book describes both the first wave of the AIDS epidemic in the Bronx and the gradual process by which I also became aware of my own unfinished business. Absorbed in the pain and losses of my patients and their families, I slowly began to acknowledge the grief that I had carried unknowingly for decades following the sudden death—and apparent suicide—of my father when I was an infant. I came to see how this defining event in my life had become a family secret that was never discussed, almost as if it had never happened. I came to realize how inexorably this history had led me exactly to where I had arrived, at the heart of the AIDS epidemic.

I also learned to recognize how much I had shared, unknowingly, with my patients and their families: like AIDS, suicide is something that stigmatizes both those who die and those who survive, something that is shrouded with shame, guilt, and secrecy. It disrupts everything in its wake, yet cannot be acknowledged or even named, for fear of further tainting the survivors with its stigma. All too often, for both conditions, the survivors must suffer in silence, unable to heal their wounds. Like AIDS, suicide is a terrible anomaly in the natural cycle of human life, killing young adults before their time. No wonder my patients' stories were so compelling to me; no wonder I tried so hard to shield them from their pain, which I could not do any more than I could keep my own from surfacing.

Rediscovering my history led me to realize how I had become over-identified with my work and my patients, leaving less and less time for my family, as an unconscious reaction to the loss of my father. It took me years of being surrounded by drug-addicted patients with AIDS before I appreciated how my relationship to work paralleled theirs to heroin—it was a way to feel whole and keep out the pain, often at the expense of those who were closest to me. It took me years to realize that no matter how hard I tried, no matter how accomplished or prominent I became in my work, I was no more able to rescue my patients from their fate than I had been able to rescue my father from his. It took me equally long to realize that, no matter how many patients I helped survive a little longer before they died, there was nothing I could do to bring him back.

Surrounded by dying young parents, I slowly came to understand, for the first time in my life, what it meant to have a father, and to be one. This process of awakening led me to come to terms with my personal history, along with the stigma and the family secrets that it had engendered, and finally, with my own role as a son, as a husband, as a father to two young children, and as a physician. It was, for me, a journey of healing in the midst of the epidemic, a reclaiming of life in the midst of death.

I hope that this book will be of interest not only to professionals working in the AIDS field and others who have been personally touched by the epidemic, but also to a broader audience. The issues raised are relevant for all of us. Indeed, part of what made this history so compelling for me, both as a participant and an observer, was the way in which I came to see the universality of human experience in the particularity of my patients' daily struggles. The lives that I came to know, the struggles I witnessed, were not only engrossing in themselves but also gripping in their relevance to my own life. As one patient told me, "AIDS is kind of like life, just speeded up"—and, as Elisabeth Kübler-Ross has said, "Nobody gets out of this life alive." We all have to confront the same challenges, to come to terms finally with our lives, deaths, and losses, but AIDS lends an urgency to these issues that highlights them in dramatic clarity.

If there is any hidden benefit to this devastating epidemic—and one has to look hard to find any—it may be that by framing these issues so clearly, AIDS may help lead to greater self-awareness, acceptance, and healing, both for people affected by it and for their care providers. Like any life-threatening illness or challenge, only more intensely, AIDS offers us the opportunity to go through fear, pain, and darkness and come out on the other side. Recognizing the darkness and passing through it is a prerequisite for anyone seeking to be an effective caregiver: otherwise it will always remain an unconscious barrier, something which stands in the way of our being truly present.

In its first decade, AIDS was like a clear, harsh light, stripping away pretense, conceit, and the youthful illusion that life will go on forever. It united patients and their caregivers in humble solidarity: if they could not stop the disease, they could at least promise to accompany each other through it. It was in this role of witness and companion that I discovered the true and most important role of the physician.

Now the eagerly awaited therapeutic era for AIDS has begun. In sharp contrast to the first decade of the epidemic in the Bronx, when all we could do was bear witness and walk side by side with our patients through their illness, AIDS has now been rendered a treatable disease, albeit still incurable. This is something for which I am very grateful as a clinician. I only hope, however, that this does not lead to a loss of that unmediated human connection between patients and care providers, as the technical complexity of HIV therapeutics begins to permeate the patient-physician relationship, as physicians are tempted to take refuge from their own anxieties about life and death behind the familiar thicket of machines, pharmacology, and laboratory tests.

I cannot fully predict what future course the AIDS epidemic will take, or exactly where my own involvement in it will lead me. I do know, however, that I cannot, in retrospect, imagine a different or more appropriate path for myself than the one that has brought me this far. This book charts the beginning of my own journey through the AIDS epidemic, and the process of personal awakening that began along the way. I offer it to the reader not as a guide but rather as one traveler's story among many. I hope that it may resonate in some way with your own.

*Surviving the Fall*

# 1 Immersion

What struck me most in the beginning were all the fathers dying young. First in ones and twos, then in swelling numbers, the succession of thirty-five-year-olds came into the hospital, struggled briefly, and died. They succumbed to pneumonia or other infections, or else simply wasted away, while their wives and small children came and went, walking in disbelief through white-glared hospital corridors. Suddenly and without precedent, young families were being cruelly and abruptly destroyed, with no apparent logic or warning. AIDS, though we did not know it in the summer of my medical internship in 1981, had come to the Bronx with a vengeance.

I remember Gabriel, my first patient with AIDS, a thirty-five-year-old Puerto Rican intravenous drug user whom I met in August 1981. By the time I first saw him, he had already made several trips to our hospital's emergency room for a persistent cough and shortness of breath. Each time he had been given a prescription for oral antibiotics and sent home. He was treated for what was believed initially to be bronchitis, then pneumonia. When he returned one week later by ambulance, in respiratory failure, he was so short of breath that he could not complete a sentence without gasping for air. He was wheeled by stretcher into the emergency room, imploring us with frightened eyes to save him, as his wife and five-year-old daughter hovered anxiously nearby. We admitted him to the intensive care unit and, thinking that he had severe bacterial pneumonia, treated him with strong intravenous antibiotics, which had no effect over the next forty-eight hours. Finally, as his condition became more critical, he underwent a bronchoscopy, which revealed that he had *Pneumocystis carinii* pneumonia, or PCP, a rare "opportunistic" infection that occurred only in patients with severely weakened immune systems.

We had seen several cases of PCP in drug users in our hospital, and they had resembled cases of *Pneumocystis* in young gay men that had begun cropping up in New York and California. During that summer Gerald Friedland—now my friend and colleague—had, like myself, come to the Bronx from Boston. I had met Jerry while I was in medical school at Harvard, where he had been a popular junior faculty member. Coincidentally, in the summer of my internship he came to Montefiore Hospital as an attending physician and infectious disease specialist in the Department of Internal Medicine. Soon after his arrival in the Bronx, Jerry and some of his infectious disease colleagues began noticing that cases of unexplained immunodeficiency and unusual infections were beginning to surface among intravenous drug users, with features very similar to those described in gay men.

Jerry recalls a conversation from late 1981, when he went to attend a conference in Manhattan given by an official of the Centers for Disease Control (CDC) who had come to give a talk on this new immunodeficiency syndrome. He tells of running down the hall to catch the CDC speaker after the meeting and describing the clinical features of cases such as Gabriel's that were appearing in the Bronx. When Jerry suggested that this could be the same phenomenon being found in gay men, he was promptly rebuffed. This syndrome, the CDC official assured him, occurred *only* in homosexual men: our drug-using patients must be affected by something else. One year later, in late 1982, CDC released its first report specifically identifying intravenous drug users as an AIDS risk group.

Gabriel's condition worsened, despite our initial therapy for PCP, and his blood oxygen levels dropped so low that he needed to be intubated and put on a ventilator. At that time, in order to obtain pentamidine, a potent intravenous medication specifically used to treat *Pneumocystis,* one had to make a special request to CDC, which was the only source of this drug in the United States. (Indeed, it was in part because of the increasing requests for pentamidine that CDC investigators had been led to examine these apparent clusters of *Pneumocystis carinii* pneumonia in young men in New York and California.) We called Atlanta, and the medication was shipped out by Federal Express overnight.

Gabriel improved slightly after being intubated and placed on the new medication, but he soon began to have complications from abnormal blood clotting, as well as kidney failure related to the toxic effects of pentamidine. (The drug is often effective but just as often produces serious side effects.) As his organ systems began to fail, one by one, Gabriel remained lucid, begging us to do something to keep him alive, but we ultimately realized that we were powerless to do so.

One morning, after ten days in intensive care, his heart stopped beating. A "code" was called: the familiar hospital drill in which a special resuscitation team swiftly converges on the patient's room after cardiac arrest. But by the time the unit staff had donned all the protective gear—

gowns, gloves, and masks, the degree of isolation seeming to escalate as his condition worsened—and had assembled in Gabriel's room, his pupils were fixed and dilated.

Shaken, I went out to see his wife. She was leaning against the wall for support, moaning and sobbing. Next to her stood her daughter, quiet and wide-eyed, twirling her braids distractedly. I was struck with the finality of the moment: Gabriel's wife seemed too young to be a widow, his daughter too young to have to spend the rest of her life without her father. I talked with the wife for a few minutes, feeling uncomfortable and inarticulate, and then watched them both walk slowly off the floor, out into the balmy Bronx night, side by side, alone with their pain.

When I think back on it now, more than fifteen years later, Gabriel's face merges with the faces of hundreds of others of my patients who have since died of AIDS. Still, I cannot forget his eyes, and their final appeal, which I was unable to honor. For me, like his biblical namesake, Gabriel was a herald of things to come, the harbinger of an era that at the time I could only dimly imagine.*

I recall another summer night in the Bronx, almost a decade later, when I made a detour on my way home to go to a patient's wake. From the handwritten message that I had been given, I saw that the funeral home was in an unfamiliar section of the East Bronx. I located the street address on my Bronx borough atlas and eventually found it, near an intersection known as a heavy drug-use area close to Crotona Park. The funeral home was one of the few buildings still occupied on the block. It was flanked by abandoned, boarded-up brownstones; across the street was a rubble-strewn vacant lot.

---

*With this one exception, all patients' names in this book have been changed. Certain details of patients' life circumstances have also been changed.

I parked in front and walked into the dimly lit foyer. Unlike some of the larger funeral homes I had been to, which often had simultaneous functions going on—curiously reminiscent of adjacent wedding parties at a large catering facility—this one had only one visitation room, its door near the back of the foyer. I went in and sat for a few minutes in back, taking in the scene. There were only a couple of people there. Candles were burning, the room flickered with shadows, and the open casket was surrounded with flowers. A police siren pierced the silence and, moments later, the flashing red light of a patrol car shone through an outside window and played briefly on the wall.

I stood up to approach the casket, and as I walked down the central aisle to the front of the room, I thought back on my last conversations with Valerie, my patient who had died. I recalled her wit and good humor, and her losing struggle to stay alive. For a long time she had fought hard against death, mostly to be there for her eleven-year-old daughter. Then, when she was too tired to fight any longer, she simply let go.

I stopped in front of the coffin, lowered my head, and looked down: to my astonishment, the body in the coffin was not Valerie's—a black woman in her forties—but that of a young, hollow-cheeked Hispanic man, who looked to be in his late twenties. I gasped, felt dizzy, and stood there for a moment. I noted the dark humor of the moment, which Valerie would have appreciated. Then, speculating that this young man might also have died of AIDS, I had the sinking realization that this scenario was no doubt being enacted that night in the funeral parlors of forgotten neighborhoods throughout the city, as grieving families stood before the caskets of their dead: all the young adults, parents, children, husbands, wives, brothers, and sisters all having come to this end, all connected by the precise aim of one search-and-destroy virus.

Silently I wished safe passage to this young man's soul and discreetly left the room. After making a call from the office outside, I learned that there had been a miscommunication: Valerie was indeed being laid out in a funeral home that night, but I had been told the wrong one—she was all the way on the other side of the Bronx, off Valentine Avenue near Burnside. I got into my car and drove across the wide reaches of the darkened borough—passing by how many other similar local scenes, I wondered—until I found my destination. Entering the chapel of the funeral home, seeing Valerie's mother and daughter both bent over her casket sobbing, I knew, sadly, that I had arrived in the right place.

There were countless small and momentous ways in which everything in my life led to my arriving in the right place, as a physician in the midst of the AIDS epidemic. Most of this journey was unconscious, and at times I felt as though I was lost, but was drawn toward that destination as unerringly as if I were reading a map. It was only after I had already gotten there that I fully realized where I had been going, and why. As with most journeys, however, arriving at my destination also meant coming home. These remembrances chart the course of my homecoming.

My road to the AIDS epidemic began in the spring of 1954, when I was born in Flushing Hospital, in the borough of Queens, in New York City. I was the first child my parents had longed for, after several miscarriages. We lived for a brief time in a garden apartment in Fresh Meadows. My father died suddenly when I was a baby, in the fall of 1955, too early for me to have any conscious memories of him.

When I was old enough to ask questions about my father's death, I was told that he had fallen accidentally out of a window in a tall building downtown. Implausible as it seems, I imagine either that this simple explanation made enough sense for me to accept it, or else after a while I just stopped asking when no other details were forthcoming. Any questions I might have had about my father's life before he died were met with equally sketchy information. As a consequence, I was left with both a void and a mystery, yet I remained unconscious of anything actually lacking in my life. Not until I had been confronted with the deaths of hundreds of young fathers in the AIDS epidemic did I realize that there was more to the story about my father and his death than I had grown up believing. Not until I had witnessed the effects of all my patients' premature deaths on their survivors did I realize how bereft I was of an emotional legacy from my own father.

Soon after my father died, my mother and I moved into Manhattan, and I grew up an only child on the upper West Side. I was a good boy, perhaps too good, shy but popular, and I have mostly happy memories of childhood. I went to the Ethical Culture schools through high school, graduating from Fieldston in 1972. (My grandparents, first-generation Russian Jews, had become stalwarts of the Ethical Culture Society, a nondenominational humanist association founded in New York in 1876.) I chose to go to Swarthmore College because of its academic reputation and its Quaker tradition—and because a cousin of mine who I thought was really cool went there. I dabbled in the counterculture of the sixties and early seventies, but I always did everything I was supposed to do, and did it well. I graduated with highest honors in 1976 from Swarthmore, where I majored in history, philosophy, and the Grateful Dead. A year later, I started medical school.

This is the bare outline of my life up to my mid-twenties. Many of the early details, particularly concerning my father's death and its meaning for my life, would not be filled in until many years later, illumined by the piercing light of the AIDS epidemic.

My decision to go to medical school was not based on a great love or even familiarity with biology or other natural sciences. It evolved instead from the political context of the 1960s antiwar movement and its aftermath, in which having a concrete skill and being of service were important values. Like many in my generation, I came to political awareness during the Vietnam War and the civil rights movement and was accustomed to thinking of my individual life decisions—perhaps somewhat grandiosely—in terms of their political and social impact.

I decided to become a doctor during a semester abroad in Paris, in my sophomore year of college. Until then, I had planned to be an actor, or a playwright, or a history professor, and had never taken any college science courses—I probably even took a measure of pride in this fact. Away from home, far from my familiar surroundings, I had an experience that radically changed my plans for what I would do with my life.

I got to Paris in January 1974, a few months before my twentieth birthday. The housing rental market was difficult, and I did not have a lot of money, but I managed to find a small room in a decrepit building in the Fifth Arrondissement, on the Rue de la Montagne Ste. Genevieve. It was the first time that I had lived so far away from home. I felt very lonely and uprooted—feelings that were further compounded by the absence of TV, radio, stereo, or telephone in my room—and more on my own than I could recall ever feeling. I experienced something akin to what I later learned in anthropology courses was a "liminal" process, in which adolescent boys in certain tribal societies who are to be initiated into manhood are first separated from everything that has defined them as boys, in order to be symbolically re-created as men.

Several weeks after I arrived, I spent a lonely Saturday night in my little room, drinking cheap wine and reading a French newspaper report about continuing atrocities by the junta in Chile. The Pinochet coup had occurred in fall 1973, culminating in the death of the elected President Salvador Allende. This event had had a great impact on me and my circle of friends at Swarthmore, as a chilling example of how truth and justice did not always prevail in the real world. As I lay there on the bed reading, I was suddenly overwhelmed by all the cruelty and meanness in the world:

I felt very vulnerable, like a little boy lost in a hostile and dangerous adult world. I did not relate this feeling to my own personal history, to the fact that I had grown up without a father; rather, I experienced it as a nonspecific feeling of rootlessness, a vaguely sick feeling of being adrift in the world, needing something to protect me from the threats that lurked everywhere in this menacing, grown-up environment.

Just as suddenly and unexpectedly, I felt the strong impulse to go to medical school and become a doctor, something that I had never consciously considered before. Medicine—the image of a wise, skillful, near-omnipotent physician coming to me as if in a vision—would be a shield, a way to protect myself as I took the step from boyhood to manhood. Medicine would give me a skill, something that would help define who I was. Although this impulse was sudden and irrational—and I was used to approaching things in my life with careful planning—it was strong enough, and persistent enough, that upon my return home in the fall I enrolled in my first premed courses at Swarthmore.

This vision of the physician representing technical competence, capability, and power over disease and death, would be sorely challenged less than a decade later by the emergence of the AIDS epidemic. My truest skills as a physician eventually came from being a witness, a companion, a facilitator rather than an all-powerful conqueror of illness, shielded against the pain of the world. But I have never regretted that impulsive decision to become a doctor.

I enrolled at Harvard Medical School in 1977, at the tail end of the post-war *pax antibiotica*, when it seemed only a matter of time before all human diseases would be brought under the dominion of medical science, whose authority seemed limitless. Over the next four years, little emerged to challenge this complacent worldview. When I entered medical school, I envisioned myself working in a health center in a poor urban community after my training, combining medical skills with political activism.

Medical school itself, especially the first two classroom years in Harvard's imposing amphitheaters, did not undermine this commitment, although it was difficult to maintain perspective while immersed in the unfamiliar environment of biochemistry, physiology, and histology. Once I started my clinical rotations in Boston's hospitals, I learned that there was a human dimension to society and behavior that my political worldview, steeped in Swarthmore's seminar rooms, had not comprehended.

Even before I began medical school, I had decided that I would pursue residency training in family medicine, for it seemed to me that this specialty—which embraced generalism as its basic principle—was best suited to understanding and helping people in the context of their lives, families, and communities. My early clinical experience served only to reinforce the appropriateness of that choice for my training. My goal, to pursue family medicine training and then work as a community physician in a poor, inner-city area, was not always congruent with the outlook of the administration at Harvard Medical School, several of whose members suggested to me that I was throwing away a perfectly good medical education by wanting to take up family practice in the Bronx. At the time, I stuck to my decision out of a combination of willfulness, defiance, and pride. I wouldn't have been able to articulate fully why I wanted to pursue this path, particularly its focus on the family, but I applied and was accepted into the family medicine residency program at Montefiore Medical Center in the Bronx, to begin in summer 1981.

Several weeks before starting internship, my fiancée and I got married. Nancy and I had met on the first day of medical school, and we immediately became friends. We both felt somewhat alienated from the trappings of academic medicine—she had studied fine arts in college and had supported herself for several years as a painter before starting medical school, while I had worked for a year after college as a nursing assistant in the operating rooms at Massachusetts General Hospital. We instantly gravitated toward each other. Nancy was warm, outgoing, and emotionally present, whereas I was reserved and cerebral and had a tendency to escape into intellectual distractions, yet somehow we formed a close bond that enabled us to support each other through medical school.

Although we started out as friends, our relationship intensified during our first-year anatomy course. We were cadaver mates in dissection class, and our own intimacy progressed as we crossed new thresholds of intimacy with the body we were dissecting. Our anatomy class became both a personal and professional rite of passage. By the end of the year we had finished our dissection and were all but living together.

It was a challenge to continue to develop and maintain our relationship during the next few years of medical school, with all the competing demands on our time and attention, and these challenges persisted through residency and beyond. Being on call, going without sleep, studying for hours without a break, giving so much of ourselves to our patients and the demands of work—the realities of our daily lives often left us with little time or attention to give to each other. Still, when we were able to get past these work-related distractions—and this remains true today—we found a deep connection that neither of us had previously experienced.

In our last year of medical school we decided to get married, fitting in the wedding and a rushed honeymoon to Nantucket between graduation and the beginning of internship in July. Nancy had enrolled in the pediatrics track in the same residency program where I was about to start at Montefiore, and, just back from our honeymoon, we both immersed ourselves in our training, rarely seeing each other.

❋

In the summer of 1981, the world at large did not yet seem to be very much affected by what would soon become known as AIDS. A couple of reports had just appeared in the *New England Journal of Medicine* and the Centers for Disease Control's *Morbidity and Mortality Weekly Report*, documenting clusters of *Pneumocystis carinii* pneumonia and Kaposi's sarcoma among young homosexual men in New York and California, but this seemed merely to be a further elaboration on what had been derisively referred to as "gay bowel syndrome" or "gay-related immunodeficiency syndrome" (GRID), peculiarities described in the medical literature within the previous couple of years. It was not evident to CDC at the time, and certainly not to me, that this new disease was about to exert profound effects on patterns of life and death in many at-risk communities across the country. In 1981, when people died it still happened in the conventional way: death was usually expected, and those dying were generally either very old or very young.

My first set of patients that summer consisted mostly of elderly men and women from nearby communities in the Bronx or local nursing homes. These patients were admitted to Montefiore with the kinds of illnesses I was accustomed to treating during my medical school training: congestive heart failure, coronary artery disease, urinary tract infections, strokes, diabetes, and peripheral vascular disease. Mostly Jewish, Italian, and Irish, with a smaller proportion of blacks and Hispanics, these patients seemed like so many surrogate great aunts, uncles, and grandparents. Gabriel's case of *Pneumocystis* pneumonia was a distinct exception to this pattern; he and the few other young adult patients admitted to the hospital with complications of drug abuse or acute bacterial pneumonias that summer had not yet come to redefine the quality and substance of medical care in our hospital's inpatient medicine service. Anyone who had stopped to notice might have seen a couple of metal carts with disposable protective gear in the corridors, outside the rooms of the few patients who had been put on isolation precautions for infectious diseases, but these hardly seemed to attract anyone's attention—certainly not mine as I scurried from room to room with the frantic pace of a harried intern.

That summer, my grandfather became ill and died at the age of ninety-two. My mother's father, he had come to this country from Russia with his family in 1892, arriving at Ellis Island as a small boy of three. He grew up on the Lower East Side, one of eight siblings, went to Townsend Harris High School and City College, became a dentist, and opened a dental office in Flatbush, Brooklyn, where he lived and worked for more than forty years. He and my grandmother, who had been a schoolteacher, moved into Manhattan to live in an apartment next door to my mother and me the year after my father died.

My grandfather often took me for walks in Central Park, to the carousel, the skating rink, or the zoo. After I started school he often came to pick me up and walk me home in the afternoon. When I was a little older, he helped to instill in me values of social justice and the importance of helping other people and doing good work in the world. My grandfather was a lifelong democratic socialist—I recall many heated debates at his kitchen table with his brother Sidney, who was a communist—and the walls of his apartment were filled with portraits of his heroes: Eugene V. Debs, Norman Thomas, FDR, Martin Luther King, and the Ethical Culture leaders Henry Neumann and John Lovejoy Elliott. I remember once walking with him down Ninth Avenue when I was nine or ten, carrying a couple of grocery bags full of canned goods that we were bringing to a drop-off point in the theater district, where one of the Broadway stage unions was collecting donations for civil rights protesters in Mississippi and Alabama. It felt good to be walking next to him, feeling the weight of my brown paper bag and a sense of importance about what we were doing; I also felt a little apprehensive about the bad things he told me were happening down south, but his being with me made it seem safe. If there was any constant male presence in my life as I was growing up, my grandfather was it, and he filled this role admirably.

I often marveled at what it must have been like for my grandfather to witness the entire span of the twentieth century and the vast changes that had occurred during his lifetime. I was always very close to him, even during the seven or eight years before his death, when a stroke had left him unable to communicate and his energy and strength slowly dwindled. During his last illness he became progressively weaker at home, stopped eating, drifted in and out of consciousness, and was finally hospitalized after developing pneumonia. I recalled from medical school the term used for pneumococcal pneumonia in the preantibiotic era: "The old man's friend."

He was hospitalized in a four-bed open ward at St. Vincent's Hospital in Manhattan. The place had the appearance of not having changed much since the 1930s: old metal beds with tubular frames, yellow tiled walls, and two large ceiling fans stirring lazily overhead. He shared the room with a Puerto Rican man in his fifties who was there for a bleeding stomach ulcer, a young black transvestite with pneumonia—probably, in retrospect, an early, unnoticed case of AIDS—and a benign and stoic Native American from Hell's Kitchen named Danny, who suffered from nonhealing diabetic foot ulcers. I was pleased that Danny had the bed next to my grandfather; whenever I left it always seemed that Danny's calm and wise presence surrounded him with safety. The transvestite was also very pleasant and helpful. Often Sage would go down to the coffee shop to get sandwiches for us, in between trying out new dance routines, listening intently to the Temptations on an old tape player.

The night my grandfather finally died, I knew that I would not see him alive again, and I stood by his bed in a somewhat awkward mixture of grandson and physician-in-training, the physician in me making note of certain signs (pulse, respirations, level of consciousness) but not wanting to interfere with the grandson in me who needed to be there, too. I told him that I loved him, that I knew he loved me, and that I would always carry him in my heart. Even though he had not been talking or interacting with people in the preceding few days, he turned his head toward me and squeezed my hand. I kissed him, stroked his hair, and said goodbye. Early the next morning, we got a call from the hospital that he had died.

Sad as it was, there seemed to be something appropriate about his death, and while I carried a wistful sorrow with me for the rest of the summer, I was satisfied that I had been able to be with him and have that last exchange. My sadness was made more poignant by my work with elderly patients that summer, as I began to see each one of them as someone's grandparent, spouse, or even child. Nevertheless, there was still something fitting about all of this, something that made sense about our work in the hospital, as we helped the elderly either to live with dignity or die when their time had come. Our worldview, our sense of what defined the role and capabilities of the physician, had not yet been transformed by the prospect of death's coming so fiercely to the younger generation.

I did not return to the medicine ward at Montefiore, where I had spent that first summer, until almost a year later, because I was occupied doing rotations on other services. On my return, I was surprised to notice that the rows of patient charts in the racks, whose spines had previously been marked with names like Goldberg, Mazzacco, and O'Brien, now largely bore such names as Diaz, Rivera, and Williams. Looking down the hallways, the metal carts had multiplied; now it seemed almost as if every other room had an isolation cart outside the door.

In June 1981, when I graduated medical school, I had no idea, nor do I think anyone could have known, that before the end of the decade, AIDS would become the leading cause of death for both men and women aged twenty-five to forty-four in the United States and in many capital cities around the world. I would have been shocked if someone had told me at my graduation, as I sat thinking I had acquired the knowledge that would be the foundation of my medical practice, that this disease would not only be the major focus of my work as a physician but also that it would be un-treatable and rapidly fatal during much of the first decade of its epidemic spread.

My simple notion of having a useful skill and being of service was to be confronted by a disease that fundamentally shattered the illusion that med-icine and science could control any disease, almost as if by willing it. Be-ing involved with the epidemic as it unfolded often meant having one's ba-sic identity and self-esteem as a physician challenged to the core. But for the moment, as I began my residency training, the tools I had acquired in medical school seemed adequate for the tasks at hand.

During my internship and residency, I immersed myself in the family practice training program, going from one hospital service to the next: in-ternal medicine, pediatrics, obstetrics. I also began an outpatient practice, which was part of the training program, in Montefiore's Family Health Center near Fordham Road, in the mid-Bronx, where I soon acquired a substantial patient panel. This immersion in medical training, and in the lives and cultures of the people in this Bronx community, was very grati-fying.

I often felt a sense of privilege and wonder at being brought into peo-ple's lives, being able to witness and be part of their dramas, struggles, and life experiences. I began to appreciate the richness that lies beneath the sur-face of even the most seemingly ordinary lives, something that I had not experienced in other settings. I came to love my patients and was gratified by their loyalty to me as well. These are just a few of the many patients that memory brings easily to mind:

• Mrs. Montalvo was a Puerto Rican cleaning woman in her fifties, who worked nights as a housekeeper cleaning the offices of an insurance company in a big building downtown. She made enough money to support herself and her retarded adult son and carried herself with a style, poise, and grace that I had rarely seen. She was particularly proud of her ability to keep her skin soft and smooth despite the rigors of her job, using a carefully selected combination of creams, emollients, and home remedies. I remember her once giggling like a schoolgirl when she described her budding relationship with a man, who had recently arrived from her hometown near Ponce. He was courting her, she confided, in the slow, "old fashioned" way, and she was concerned lest he think her attraction to him too brazen. . . .

• Miss Marsh, a very proper retired schoolteacher and maiden aunt of a well-to-do black family from Charleston, South Carolina, could hardly walk due to severe arthritis and peripheral vascular disease. She always made her clinic visits dressed in a clean pressed blue suit, with a matching hat, a lace blouse, and white gloves. She walked slowly with a gnarled wooden cane and needed help getting in and out of a chair. In a measured, polite voice she exchanged pleasantries with the staff, and on occasion she described the indignities of living in a deteriorating building off the Grand Concourse. In her small apartment, near the once-majestic avenue that had been modeled on the *grands boulevards* of Paris, she was often a virtual prisoner, having to stay inside all day, either to avoid being harassed by the drug dealers or because the elevator had broken and she was unable to negotiate the stairs. Through it all, she never lost her composure. . . .

• Mrs. Bartlett, an imposing black woman in her forties who looked to be in her sixties, had raised five children on welfare, while going to secretarial school and organizing a tenants' rights organization in her building. In the five years that I knew her she had a stroke, a heart attack, a foot amputation because of diabetic small-vessel disease and gangrene, and a hysterectomy for massive uterine bleeding. Somehow, with each affront to her physical integrity she seemed to grow stronger, more solid. Through this entire sequence of misfortunes, she remained calm and cheerful, always taking time at her clinic visits to thank me for my efforts on her behalf—which from my perspective, sometimes seemed liked a losing battle—saying that she was happy to bear whatever God had in store for her. . . .

• The Pengs, a three-generation family of recently arrived Cambodian refugees, lived in the apartment building directly across the street from the health center. Like many other families we soon encountered, this one had unceremoniously arrived here as the result of political turmoil in the 1970s in postwar Southeast Asia and the availability of cheap housing in the poor outer boroughs of New York City. None of us had even been aware of the Cambodian refugees that had been recently resettled in New York—and in particular in this Bronx neighborhood, where they had been placed by immigrant relocation agencies—until one day when a nurse practitioner from the clinic saw a sick-looking child with a runny nose sitting on the stoop of the building across the street and coaxed the child and his family into the center. Word quickly spread, and before long we had a substantial population of Cambodian and other Southeast Asian patients; the center soon hired a young Cambodian woman, herself a recent immigrant, to act as translator and patient advocate. The Pengs were always cordial and deferential—bowing when they entered and left the exam room, bringing me carefully wrapped little gifts at holiday time—and they were devoted to their four children. With pained ambivalence they witnessed their older sons' assimilation into the fast-paced culture of their new city. I was always reminded of the limits of cross-cultural medicine, particularly when one doesn't know the language, when I asked what I thought was a simple question, and an animated five-minute discussion ensued between Avi, the translator, and the older Pengs. Avi turned back to me, smiling sweetly, and said simply, "No." . . .

• Angela and Rico were an earnest young couple expecting their first child. She was seventeen, from a large Italian family in Morris Park. She had left home and Catholic school to move in with Rico, a handsome Puerto Rican young man from Tremont, three years her senior. After they lived together for a year in Rico's room in his mother's apartment, Rico managed to get a steady entry-level job with the city transit authority, which meant security and enough money for them to get their own apartment. They both came to every prenatal visit, often arriving an hour ahead of time in eager anticipation, presenting me with overflowing lists of questions about how to prepare for the baby, what types of food would be good for Angela to eat, what kind of diapers they should get, whether they could keep having sex during the pregnancy. I still have not seen anything to equal the rapture in their eyes when, following a long and difficult labor, during which Rico never left Angela's side, I handed them their healthy newborn in the delivery room. . . .

• Mrs. Sullivan, a frail eighty-five-year-old Irish woman with pale, almost transparent skin, bed bound with diabetic foot ulcers, whom I saw for home visits in her fifth floor walk-up on Decatur Avenue, lived around the corner from the health center. Her husband had died years before, and she lived with her sixty-year-old daughter, herself a widow, who went down for provisions to the corner grocery store every day, wheeling her collapsible wire cart, scarf tied firmly around her head. Stepping into the apartment was like entering a time warp: behind the battered metal door just like all the others in the building were lace curtains, upholstered sofa and chairs with doilies neatly pinned in place, wood-framed mirrors, and an old black-and-white television set. It all evoked the 1940s rather than the 1980s. A photograph of Mrs. Sullivan's son, proud and handsome in his military uniform, was displayed on the mantelpiece, forty years after his death in the Battle of the Bulge. I often wondered what Mrs. Sullivan, who lit-

erally had not been out of her house in decades, would think if she
were to be brought downstairs, or even next door, to see how the
neighborhood had been transformed, while for her time had been
standing still. . . .

Beyond the life stories of all my individual patients, I had the satisfying
feeling of coming to appreciate the texture and fabric of life in certain
Bronx inner-city communities. The area just north of Fordham Road near
the clinic, traditionally Irish, had become predominantly Puerto Rican
and black, with enclaves of recent arrivals from Guyana, Central America and Cambodia. I became familiar with the bodegas and botánicas of
the neighborhood around the Family Health Center, learning about some
of the medicinal herbs that my patients used as well as about food and
spices. I often stopped by on my way to clinic and pick up some pasteles or
empanadas for lunch, or to buy some fresh cilantro (which had not yet in-
vaded restaurant menus coast to coast) to experiment with at home. I can
still remember the velvet, caramel-sugar sweetness of the flan that Señora
Diaz, a spry ninety-two-year-old who described herself, laughing, as my
"Puerto Rican grandmother," brought me from time to time. I had learned
to speak Spanish in medical school and, in preparation for coming to work
in "El Bronx," I had spent several months in my fourth year working in a
rural health clinic in Puerto Rico. Once I started working at the Family
Health Center, I began to accumulate a growing number of Spanish-
speaking patients; many days I spoke more Spanish than English during
my clinic sessions.

Just a few blocks away, on Arthur Avenue in the Little Italy section of
the Bronx, Italian butcher shops, bakeries, restaurants, churches, and religious bookstores were lined up in orderly succession. Italian grandmothers sat out on the stoop on summer nights, dressed in black; next to

them were their grizzled, gray-haired husbands, wearing sleeveless undershirts. I discovered that the restaurants on Arthur Avenue were one of the Bronx's best-kept secrets, and I went regularly to Mario's or Dominic's for meals that rivaled any to be found downtown, without the wait and at two-thirds the cost. Jerome Avenue, closer to Montefiore, had Schweller's, Epstein's, and Katz's delicatessens, with salamis and hot dogs hanging in the window, knishes on the front grill, the steamed-up fluorescent Hebrew National signs, and big jars of pickled peppers. Here it was easy to feel transported to an earlier, more benign time. The numbers tattooed on the forearm of one of the countermen at Schweller's, a Holocaust survivor, served as a more ominous reminder of years past.

This was the "other" New York, the New York of the outer boroughs, the places where few tourists ever come, and which seem even to some natives of the city outside the gates of the "real" New York. Growing up in Manhattan, I shared this prejudice, and even after traveling the subway to school in Riverdale for six years, I had never set foot in any other part of the Bronx. (Indeed, although part of the Bronx according to the city map, Riverdale, with well-kept middle-class homes and apartment buildings the rule and with some neighborhoods of luxury mansions, had much more in common with Scarsdale than it did with the Bronx communities that I was discovering.)

Some nights when I was on call at North Central Bronx Hospital, the city hospital affiliated with Montefiore, I took the elevator up to the top floor, which had a panoramic view of the streets below. Gazing out at the darkened landscape and twinkling lights, I was overwhelmed and excited by the thought that I was on the lookout, ready to deal with whatever medical catastrophes the Bronx had to offer that night. (I was one of the "liaison officers of the night," as Céline wrote in another context, describing the working women of Montmartre.) Occasionally, I looked across the broad valley of Van Cortlandt Park to see Riverdale rising up on the other side. If I looked carefully, I could make out the shape of the Fieldston

ıry building, which had been constructed with much fanfare
ₓg my junior year in high school. The distinctive, well-lit building
looked at night like an ocean liner moored in the harbor, far removed from
the dark, swirling seas below.

I still recall one time when I was eleven years old, being stranded with
my mother on the Cross-Bronx Expressway with a flat tire. As the stream
of cars and trucks roared by endlessly, none stopping, I felt a tremendous
sense of menace and foreboding—a pre–*Bonfire of the Vanities* urban
nightmare—of being marooned forever in the middle of the Bronx. Years
later, I had a distinct feeling of pride and familiarity as I would dart on and
off the same Expressway to avoid traffic or to go from clinic to clinic in the
South Bronx, no longer a stranger in a strange land.

Just as I began to appreciate these self-contained worlds and cultures,
however, the texture of life in many of these neighborhoods began to
change irrevocably, due to a disease which had yet to be given a name. The
fabric was starting to unravel, at first in a series of anomalies or coinci-
dences, then as a systematic process of destruction that completely and
permanently altered these Bronx communities. AIDS was beginning to
leave its mark, and would continue to do so for decades to come.

Ironically, during those same years the city of New York, with the en-
dorsement of then-mayor Ed Koch, put up a series of painted trompe l'oeil
facades to cover the open windows and doors of gutted and abandoned
buildings lining the Cross-Bronx Expressway in the South Bronx. The
city's rationale was that commuters traveling the expressway from New
Jersey, Westchester County, and Connecticut, cutting through the Bronx
on their way to somewhere else, would be less alarmed by buildings that
looked inhabited. It was even suggested that putting commuters at ease
might in fact stimulate outside investment in the Bronx. (These painted
facades—with painted curtains, shutters, and even potted plants and cats
on the window sill—were so realistic that there were newspaper reports

of Bronx residents, riding by on city buses, stopping to inquire about the availability of rentals.)

This bizarre program seemed symbolic to me at the time of the two New Yorks, one pretending that the other didn't exist. Indeed, when I drove into Manhattan to visit people and neighborhoods where I had grown up, it was hard to imagine that another New York coexisted so close nearby. In the familiar surroundings of my childhood—Manhattan's upper West Side—there was no evidence, nothing to remind anyone that there was even such a thing as the Bronx. I felt this much more powerfully several years later, as AIDS began to devastate neighborhoods in the outer boroughs (as well as Harlem and the lower East Side), and yet it seemed— for a while—as if it had been covered over as effectively as those gutted buildings with the cheerfully painted facades.

After Gabriel, I began to have more patients with *Pneumocystis* or other rare infections, but at first these unusual cases did not seem in any way connected. In those early months and years it was as if strange, isolated outcroppings of disease would appear on an otherwise normal landscape. One tended to take note and then quickly return to business as usual. It wasn't until several years later that it started to become clear that there was something much more fundamental going on.

Like Rieux in Camus's *The Plague*, we watched as the first few scattered drops of rain fell, then coalesced, and gradually became a torrent which started to wear away the foundations of life in many parts of the city. The most chilling aspect of the epidemic was our realization that it had already been spreading through our vulnerable patient populations with grim efficiency, insidious and unnoticed, for four to five years.

I remember making a home visit, early in the epidemic, to see one of my first patients with AIDS, who was dying at home. José had been a strong, muscular man, working two jobs to support his family as well as his heroin habit. He had gotten into a methadone program and had stopped shooting drugs for several years before he became ill. For a while, he had done very well, holding down a job, doing some amateur boxing, and spending time with his family. Now, at the end of his all-too-brief illness, he was reduced to a stick-thin ninety pounds, as he lay bed bound at home.

The hospital bed that his family had gotten for him was too big for the small bedroom that had been converted into a sickroom, leaving little space for anything else. It accentuated his smallness. The shelves and window sills were covered with candles, pictures of saints, and other votive objects, and the slightly sweet and acrid smell of death permeated the darkened room. José's parents, two sisters, wife, and toddler-age son were all huddled next door in the living room of their cramped one-bedroom apartment. We all knew that he would soon die, and we all knew that there was nothing we could do about it. After I said my goodbyes, I walked slowly downstairs from this fourth-floor walk-up, pausing to look at the doors of the other apartments lining the stairwell, all with their chipped paint and multiple locks, each holding its own secrets. I wondered how many of these doors had similar dramas unfolding behind them.

By early 1983 it had finally been officially recognized that this new disease, which by then had been named Acquired Immunodeficiency Syndrome, or AIDS, affected not only gay men but also drug users and hemophiliacs, women and children. Epidemiologic evidence had been mounting to suggest that AIDS was most probably a blood-borne infectious disease, caused by an as yet unidentified agent. The epidemiology followed very closely that of hepatitis B virus infection, which had long been known to affect homosexual men, intravenous drug users, and blood product recipients. The notion that AIDS was caused by repeated exposure to semen and intestinal parasites in gay men was no longer a tenable hypothesis.

By the end of 1983, in a sequence of events that has been written about extensively elsewhere, scientists had identified a retrovirus initially denoted as Human T-Lymphotropic Virus-type III (HTLV-III) or Lymphadenopathy-Associated Virus (LAV). By early 1984, a test had been developed that could detect antibodies to this virus in blood specimens. In studies that were quickly replicated in many clinical sites, it was clearly shown that the great majority of patients with AIDS or what was believed to be AIDS-related illness had antibodies to this virus, while healthy comparison groups who were not felt to be at risk for this disease did not.

What was also quickly demonstrated, however, even more alarmingly, was that asymptomatic individuals belonging to the same broadly defined risk groups—homosexual or bisexual men, intravenous drug users, and hemophiliacs—also had a high prevalence of antibodies to this virus. In those early years, the significance of this was unclear. It was not known, for example, whether this indicated that these asymptomatic risk group members had been exposed but were not actively infected with the virus, or whether they were simply early in the course of their infection and had not yet shown any signs of disease. Unfortunately, and with devastating implications, the latter theory turned out to be right.

Once the blood test became available to detect antibodies to HTLV-III, a number of studies were quickly undertaken to determine the epidemiology of exposure to this newly discovered virus. Data from the first studies showed that up to 50 percent of intravenous drug users in parts of New York City had already been infected by the early 1980s, and estimates suggested that up to 5 percent of all young adults in some heavily affected neighborhoods were HIV infected. I would drive home from seeing patients at a clinic in the South Bronx and, while stopped at a traffic light observing groups of young men on the street corners, perform a mental calculus that suggested that at least one or two of them were infected. Driving past abandoned buildings, tenements, and housing projects, I wondered how many of those rooms and spaces HIV had already penetrated. More than once, I thought of *Invasion of the Body Snatchers*, imagining the silent efficiency with which this virus entered one body after the next, without its victims even being aware that they had been taken over by this invisible enemy, each conquest then becoming a source of infection for new, unsuspecting prey.

In these early years, though, before the full dimensions of the epidemic had become clear, we had the uneasy feeling that an unknown, shadowy predator was at large, ranging across the vast expanse of the Bronx, not clearly visible but leaving its distinctive tracks. I recall driving home one night, singing along with Bob Dylan's "Ballad of a Thin Man" in the cassette player: "And you know something is happening, but you don't know what it is, do you, Mr. Jones?"

As I went through my residency I continued to derive great satisfaction from coming to know and being involved in the lives of my patients. A book that had helped inspire me to go into family medicine, John Berger's *A Fortunate Man*, describes the life and work of an English country doctor who functions for the people of his village as a trusted witness to their lives—"the clerk of their records"—and as repository of the living history of the town. I felt privileged to function in this way for my patients, in some small measure. I remember feeling a mixture of pride and awkwardness when a young mother who was a recent Caribbean immigrant to the Bronx told me that she had named the baby I had delivered after me; pride because I was very touched by her gesture, awkwardness because I did not imagine that growing up with Selwyn as a first name would be a particularly enviable lot for a kid in the South Bronx. I still keep pictures, letters, and small mementos that patients gave me during those years, and

I continue now, as I did then, to place great value on patients' trust and confidence in me as their doctor.

Although I was deeply drawn into this work, there was something about it that by nature made it more overwhelming than I had expected. In Montefiore's Family Health Center, where I received my outpatient training as a resident, I would arrive for my half-day session, go to my small office and exam room, and quickly assess the stack of patient charts waiting outside my door. I would also do a quick estimate of the charts soon to be added to the pile. Each chart contained its own history, drama, and potential problems that might occupy more time than I could fairly allot to any one patient.

Seeing ten to fifteen patients in a half day and trying to do justice to all their needs turned out to be more than I could handle. I did not want to achieve greater efficiency at the price of closing my heart to my patients, and I found myself unable to keep up with the growing number of patients without starting to become mechanical or detached. One day in clinic as I struggled to keep up with one crisis after another I realized that giving care to a series of individual patients or families does not necessarily add up to giving care to a community and addressing its larger needs. It wasn't that this work wasn't important or satisfying—far from it, and indeed I have nothing but awe and respect for my friends who continue in it—but rather that I needed to find a way to deal with the larger context.

For these reasons, in late 1983 and early 1984, as I went through my final year of residency training, I began to consider other directions. I started to think of other ways in which I could have an impact on a broader population or community of people in need. Coincidentally—or, as I have become progressively more suspicious of coincidence, at exactly the right moment, for reasons I did not understand—I was offered a position to stay on at Montefiore as medical director of its drug abuse treatment program, to start in July. This was a 950-patient methadone maintenance program, with clinics in the Central and South Bronx. It had begun to provide pri-

mary medical care services for its patients and was in need of a new director to oversee the medical program.

I arranged to meet with Victor Sidel, the chairman of Montefiore's Department of Social Medicine, which administered the methadone program. At our meeting, Vic dismissed my protests of inexperience and ad-
vised me simply to consider it an opportunity for on-the-job training. I
decided to accept the position, mostly because I thought it would give me
a couple of years to decide what I really wanted to do. In July 1984, I finished my residency and took the job. Within six months I realized that instead of biding my time to decide what I really wanted to do, I had, in fact,
found it.

The day I started my new job I became the primary care doctor for nearly
one thousand patients, all of whom were current or former heroin addicts.
This was a sudden shift from the far less dysfunctional world of the Family Health Center. Any misconceptions I might have had about this were
quickly shattered when I was awakened at 2 A.M. my first night on call as
medical director of the program. I picked up the phone, sleepy-eyed, to
hear a police detective from Harlem tell me that they had just fished a man's
body out of the East River, a couple of bottles of methadone in his pocket
with my name on them, and he wanted to know if I knew anything about
it. (I didn't: all patients' methadone doses were dispensed with the medical director indicated as the prescribing physician.) I fell back to sleep
wondering what other surprises awaited me in this new world that I had
so naively entered.

We all bring our own history to our work, and I certainly brought mine,
but it is particularly important to acknowledge that this in an environment
in which one is working with drug users. The process that characterized
my first experiences with intravenous (IV) drug users (or, to use the stan-

dard current term, injection drug users), was in many ways predictable and by no means unique to me. Initially, I experienced a powerful feeling of satisfaction and self-worth, as a whole succession of HIV-infected, drug-addicted patients convinced me that I was the only person in the world who had ever understood them or could help them. It wasn't that they were being intentionally manipulative, nor that I *wasn't* probably more attentive to them than some other care providers had been. Rather, it was simply a reflection of the worldview of an entire population of drug addicts with well-developed "borderline personality" traits: on a primitive level, the caregiver is perceived as either an all-good or an all-bad parent, and for a while I could do no wrong. What more powerful way to convince a young doctor in his first job, just out of training, that he was indeed doing God's work, than to give him the explicit message that in the entire health care system of New York City he was the only person who could possibly be trusted or be of any use.

I soon learned, however, that the flip side of omnipotence is martyrdom, as I sacrificed any sense that I had needs of my own to the overriding demands of my patients. The harder I worked, the more I tried, the more my patients' needs seemed to escalate; the more I dedicated myself to my work, the more impatient and annoyed I became with any distractions from it.

This "more-committed-than-thou" high ground may bring righteous satisfaction for a while, but it is difficult to maintain. Eventually, in such situations, martyrdom often gives way to resentment, which can lead to anger, withdrawal, frustration, and burnout. This process may be accelerated if the rescuer comes across someone who does not want to be rescued, or who distrusts the rescuer's noble intentions—both of which quickly cut to the heart of the rescuer's inflated self-image. To borrow from the theoretical framework of family therapy, care providers often find themselves moving between the three sides of a triangle—the all-powerful rescuer, the helpless martyr, and the embittered perpetrator.

None of these positions is ultimately satisfying, and each takes its own toll.

Fortunately, I was able to develop a certain degree of perspective on this dynamic before I reached a point of no return from burnout and alienation. As I eventually learned, this perspective was the result of a difficult process of recognizing and coming to terms with prior losses in my own life that, without my being conscious of them, had until then been fueling some of my overinvolvement with work. Unfortunately, it took years before I was able to make this connection, but I am getting ahead of the story.

In summer 1984, three weeks after I began my new position, our first daughter, Kyra, was born. After waiting until the last year of our residency training, Nancy had become pregnant and we were both eagerly, if anxiously, looking forward to the uncharted territory of parenthood. In a motif that kept recurring for years, I became acutely aware of the compelling similarities and differences between my life and those of my patients. Many of my patients in the drug treatment program were women, some of whom I attended during pregnancy and the birth of their children. As Nancy got pregnant and gave birth to Kyra and then, two years later, to our second daughter, Casey, I sometimes shared stories with my pregnant patients about my own growing family. But then I watched helplessly as many of these women became ill and died from AIDS. Their children, too, either died or, if they were uninfected, lost their parents and went to live with extended families or in foster homes.

This seemed a cruel perversion of the normal human life cycle, as parents died before they had had a chance to parent their children. Even crueler, some of these orphaned children were also at risk of dying from the same disease, which their parents had unwittingly transmitted to them. We began to see a long succession of grandparents, weathered by their own struggles, coming forward to care for their infant grandchildren while watching their own children die of AIDS. I recall one woman in particular, Mrs. Morales, an old matriarch with a leathered face and knotted hands, who arrived in the Bronx from rural Puerto Rico just in time to see her thirty-year-old daughter, Rosa, die of disseminated tuberculosis. She had lost two other children to AIDS and drug abuse. She looked at me in mute disbelief, then asked in a puzzled voice how it could be that young people in New York City in the 1980s were dying of tuberculosis, a disease that had been eradicated in her childhood.

These grandmothers came forward like a line of weary angels, with great love and without hesitation, first to care for their dying children as they had done when they were infants, bathing them, feeding them, holding them, and then taking over the care of their grandchildren after their children's deaths. Many of them simply seemed to accept it as just another in a long succession of burdens; others saw it as God's will. For all my patients who feared that their families would reject them because of their drug use, their HIV infection, or the pain that their past behavior may have caused them, I cannot think of one case in which a grandmother did not come forward when needed. Without these women, the ripples of the epidemic would have been even more widely felt throughout the Bronx and beyond.

I did not quickly perceive the similarities, and there were certainly many differences as well, but how like these grandmothers had my own grandfather been, coming forward unhesitatingly, long after his own parenting days were over, to help care for his infant grandson who had been left abruptly without a father. Sometimes, when the grandmothers brought their surviving grandchildren in to see us in the clinic, after their children with AIDS had died, I would flash on an image of my grandfather walking me home after nursery school, as I held on to his warm, rough, and wrinkled hand. These grandmothers, for all their weariness, were eloquent examples of unconditional love; yet like my grandfather, their steady presence only underscored the absence of the parents for whom they so nobly tried to substitute.

The largest of the three methadone clinics in our drug treatment program, known simply as Unit 3, was located under the subway tracks on Jerome Avenue near Burnside, in the upper part of the South Bronx. The neighborhood was home to a busy shopping strip on Burnside, auto parts stores and "chop shops" on Jerome, as well as an equally busy street trade of drugs, sex, and other illicit merchandising. Several vacant lots and abandoned buildings—the latter often used by squatters, and later, by crack smokers—were directly across the street from the clinic's front door. The building resembled a cavernous warehouse. Simple partitions were set up to create office areas but afforded no privacy from the large waiting room.

Up until that time, the program had provided minimal on-site medical care, and there was little precedent for methadone programs to provide more. Methadone programs were traditionally set up to dispense methadone; those that had the resources also provided counseling and additional support services. In those years primary medical care was generally nonexistent, and the program doctor was often a figurehead, a role commonly filled by a semiretired physician who would come in once a week and sign methadone prescription orders. Fortunately, my predecessor at the Montefiore program had begun to develop a more substantive medical service in the several years before I arrived. Still, conditions were at first quite primitive; all this changed in response to AIDS.

The medical office in the Unit 3 clinic consisted of an eight-by-ten-foot partitioned area and an adjoining smaller room with a sink and a desk on the far side of the clinic waiting room. This was where we initiated our on-site prenatal care program and primary care service. One of the first pur-

chases I convinced the program administrator to make was a portable ultrasonic fetal stethoscope, through which we could hear the fetal heartbeat
after twenty weeks' gestation. More than once, I had to lean out of the
doorway of the cramped medical area and ask the crowd of patients in the
waiting room—who were talking, smoking, eating, and occasionally getting into fights—to keep quiet long enough for the pregnant woman inside to hear her baby's heartbeat for the first time.

Aside from the noise and commotion in the waiting room, it was common at first for patients simply to come up and start banging on the door
of the medical office, demanding to be seen. One of the few times I ever
felt physically threatened in the program was one morning when I was in
the middle of doing a pelvic examination and there was a tremendous
banging on the door, followed by violent shaking of the doorknob, which
fortunately had been locked. I went to the door and in rushed Henry, demanding to see the doctor. Henry was a barrel-chested, 250-pound black
man who was furious that his methadone take-home privileges had been
suspended because of a random urine test result that was positive for
heroin. When I told him that he had to wait, he began to raise his voice
more threateningly. Without thinking, I moved toward him and told him
in a loud, firm voice that this was a medical office, such behavior was unacceptable, and he had better return quietly to the waiting room or he
would not be seen at all. There was a moment of assessment, as there often is in such situations, and then abruptly, with a sigh like air let out of a
balloon, he stopped, looked at me, held out his hand, and apologized.

That encounter seemed to be a defining moment for our medical service. I knew at that moment that it had established itself in this unlikely
environment. I was reminded of that confrontation years later when I
went to see Henry in the hospital and joked with him about it. By that time
he was in the advanced stages of AIDS, had wasted to less than one hundred pounds, and was blind from cytomegalovirus (CMV) retinitis, a com-

mon AIDS complication that causes destructive infection of the retina. He always seemed to have a special fondness for me after that first face-off, as I did for him.

Once we had established our medical service, the patients were not only responsive but in many ways protective. More than one patient offered ominously to "take care" of any problems I might have out on the street, and patients would routinely look out for our medical staff as they made their way to and from the clinic. One time a nurse practitioner who had recently started working with us came into the clinic fuming after she had discovered that the battery had been stolen from her car parked outside. One of the patients learned of the theft, and by the end of the afternoon, the battery was back in place.

Another time I was taking care of an older patient—older by street standards, meaning someone who had survived past the age of forty-five—a stubborn but frail-looking white woman named Penny, who was forty-eight but looked to be in her sixties. Penny had survived for years on the street through a combination of stubbornness, guile, and luck. After running out of veins in her arms, she was now shooting drugs in her legs. She came in every week with fresh weeping skin ulcers on her lower extremities, made worse by the injection of cocaine and the caustic irritants with which cocaine was often adulterated, or "cut." (Adolph's Meat Tenderizer was a favored ingredient.) These ulcers often became infected and had to be treated with antibiotics; occasionally dead tissue had to be surgically removed. On this occasion, her wounds had been healing and we had been able to cover them with a protective paste bandage, which I changed every week. I was preparing to cut the bandage off and change it, rummaging in vain for a pair of scissors in the ill-equipped, makeshift medical office. I heard a distinct clicking sound, and I turned to see Penny holding the six-inch switchblade she had just pulled out from her boot. "Here, Doc," she offered, with a wide, gapped-tooth grin. "Can you use this?"

In the same office, late on a Friday afternoon in winter, I saw a patient who came in disheveled, alcohol on his breath, complaining of chest pain. Invariably it seemed that the worst disasters were reserved for Friday afternoon, as the clinic was preparing to shut down and most of the staff had already left. I opened his shirt to find a round pouch, an inch and a half wide, opening up through the skin into his chest wall, with foul-smelling pus emanating from it. "Oh yeah, Doc, that's been there for a while," he mumbled. "Didn't bother me until now." I took a flashlight and a cotton-tipped applicator, attempting to find the source of this opening, which tunneled up inside his chest, seeming to defy all anatomical explanation. *Heart of Darkness* came to mind as I probed up this blind, mysterious passage, sensing the deepening Bronx night outside. In our clinic outpost, far up-river from more familiar medical surroundings, I felt like I had crossed over into some other realm.

The more I became immersed in the epidemic, the more impatient I became with people who weren't themselves involved in it. It seemed to me that they just didn't get it, that they were intentionally ignoring something that had become the central focus of my life, and, as could be clearly seen, had become an urgent crisis for many communities in the Bronx and beyond. In part, my impatience reflected the arrogance of youth; in part, it reflected the compelling power of the epidemic, which did indeed seem to change everything in its wake.

I remember one weekend when I was covering for the Family Health Center, making hospital rounds. (This was an arrangement that I had worked out with my former family practice colleagues at Montefiore: they would cover my methadone program patients in the hospital on some weekends, and I would cover their Health Center patients on others.)

After spending most of the day making rounds, including seeing my own patients, I stopped in to see one last Health Center patient, a sixty-five-year-old man with diabetes. He was a "pre-op"—a term that, in my recent experience, I had come to associate more with transsexuals awaiting a sex change than with routine elective surgery patients—who was scheduled the next morning for an elective amputation of his left index finger at the second knuckle. He had chronic osteomyelitis, a bone infection common in diabetics that could not be adequately treated despite weeks of intravenous antibiotics. The only possible treatment was removal of the infected tissue.

As I walked in to see him, my first impression was that he was very old and markedly obese. Then I realized that this was a typical patient, very similar to the hundreds that I had cared for during medical school and residency—he looked elderly and overweight only in comparison to all my current patients who were dying in their thirties, sunken-eyed and wasted. As we talked, I realized that he was very anxious about his upcoming operation. He was tearful and sad about the anticipated loss of his finger.

Abruptly, I felt repulsed and had a strong urge to cry out, "Big fucking deal! I have a thirty-year-old patient in the next room who is going to be dead before his son's second birthday, whose wife has already died of AIDS, and you're upset about your stupid *finger?*" Of course I said nothing, and was able, I think, to offer whatever comfort and support the man needed, but I realized at that moment that I had left part of my beloved Family Health Center world behind. I have since learned that there is no true hierarchy of suffering; everyone's pain is what it is, and everyone's pain is legitimate. For a time, however, surrounded by all my dying young men, women, and children, nothing else seemed to matter to me.

We gave care to our patients in the methadone program because they came to us and we could not turn them away. Within two years, even with minimal staff in such makeshift surroundings, we saw a sharp drop in infant mortality and prematurity, and an increase in birth weights among pregnant women who received on-site prenatal care. But no sooner did this crisis appear to be resolved than another harsh drama began to be played out among those same women: mother-infant HIV transmission and the painful choices that ensued. We began to have the uneasy feeling—a feeling that was to recur often with other patients—of never quite being able to catch up to the AIDS epidemic: as soon as we responded effectively in one area, a new crisis emerged in another. To the overinvolved young medical director, every new obstacle was only an excuse to work harder, a response that brought some measure of satisfaction but also began to take a hidden toll.

From the time I started as medical director of the methadone program in 1984 until I finally left Montefiore in early 1992, we had a weekly meeting of our program medical staff. Every Thursday we gathered to talk about patient issues, problems, and strategies for dealing with the continuing onslaught of the epidemic. At first, our medical group consisted only of myself, three physician assistants who were the backbone of the program, and two quarter-time physicians, for this program of more than nine hundred IV drug–using patients. As the epidemic grew, so did our staff, and by the end of the decade we had more than tripled in size. At first, we could easily fit our weekly meetings around a small table in our program's administrative office near the hospital. Later on, we all had to squeeze together around a large table in one of the hospital library conference rooms.

Every week, as I inscribed the names in a black three-ring binder, we took account of the patients who had died during the preceding week. In the early years, these were mostly cases of patients who had suddenly gotten sick with high fever or shaking chills, shortness of breath, or seizures; they would be taken by ambulance to the hospital, where they would soon die. These patients died of pneumonia or fulminant bacterial infections,

infections that often represented their first AIDS-related illness. Later on, the deaths were more protracted, occurring after a much longer course of multiple illnesses and short periods of remission. In some cases, death actually seemed welcome after we had witnessed the progressive deterioration that left some patients emaciated, blind, incontinent, and mute from AIDS-related dementia before they finally, mercifully, succumbed.

This weekly reading of the names of the dead was eerily reminiscent of Defoe's *Journal of the Plague Year*, in which the author carefully details the weekly death counts in different London parishes during the onslaught of the Great Plague of 1665. As I carefully wrote down each patient's name, along with the date, site, and cause of death, it seemed that like Defoe we could do little more than document, in neatly arrayed rows, the fates of those who had joined the growing cadre of the dead. It literally did feel, from the perspective of our close-knit medical group, as though we were witnessing the arrival of the plague, as this continuing stream of patients became ill and died from a disease whose course we could do virtually nothing to affect. First one a month, then two, then one a week, sometimes more. In a pattern that still seems to be the case, there were periods of seeming calm, and then a deluge of four or five patients dying within a few days.

During all my years of medical school and residency training, fewer than ten patients had died while directly under my care, and all but one of them had been in their eighties or older. Now, in the methadone program, scores and eventually hundreds of patients died under my care, and not one of them was over fifty. During the years from 1984 through 1987, the death rate of patients in our methadone program—already ten times higher than that of their age-matched peers—more than tripled due to the ravages of AIDS. Most of these patients who were dying were within five years of my own age.

✳

Once during those years, we were visited by a group of French physicians and researchers. They had come to see firsthand the effects of this new plague on the South Bronx, a locale that already held great fascination for European intellectuals as a stark symbol of the disintegration of American society. After taking them on a tour of our clinics and the surrounding neighborhoods, we retired to an old Irish pub near Montefiore's main hospital complex on Gun Hill Road. Over Guinness and the unmistakably pungent aroma of Gauloises bleues, they expressed their wonderment that such devastation could exist, business-as-usual, within the same city as the glass and steel monuments of downtown Manhattan. (I didn't have to remind them of the discrepancy between the Champs Elysées and the drab Parisian *banlieues;* this was an altogether different order of magnitude.)

One of the researchers, a cultural anthropologist, observed that the worldview of some of the patients we had spoken with resembled that found in early European peasant cultures, in which the prospect of death or calamity—whether by war, famine, natural disaster, or the whim of the feudal lord—was so ever-present that it became almost mundane. It was accepted as normal in such cultures for strong, young adults to die suddenly and without warning; it was not a state of emergency, it was the way of the world.

I thought back to all the funerals I had attended, all the funeral parlors I had passed in these same neighborhoods, and the faces of all the grandparents who had come forward to care for their orphaned grandchildren, for whom death was such a familiar visitor. (In the words of the old blues song, "He'll come to your house and he won't stay long / Take another look and one of your family will be gone / Death don't have no mercy in this land.") As I reflected on this, it didn't make any of it seem less overwhelming, even if you did come to expect it. The difference, I thought, was that with AIDS this wasn't always the way of the world. AIDS was something new, it wasn't *supposed* to happen. AIDS had changed the landscape, irrevocably, but, unlike random death in those medieval peasant cultures, it had not *always* been part of that landscape. Its newness seemed to amplify its vengeance, and its power.

I recall vividly another occasion, not long after that visit, when I was given a copy of a letter that had been written to the chairman of our department at Montefiore by a local medical officer in rural Uganda. The letter was handwritten, in a careful, neat script that reminded me of a high school English composition. With chilling eloquence, the correspondent described the devastation that AIDS had brought to the villages in his province. With grim predictability, the young men became ill with "slim disease," then stopped working as fishermen or laborers; their families began to suffer from lost wages and productivity; the women became ill, either from AIDS or malnutrition; the children did the same, and were often, ultimately, orphaned. Those young adults who managed to escape the plague had left for the city, because there was no viable means of existence left in the villages, which were inexorably becoming abandoned, literally drained of their lifeblood.

The letter was a desperate plea for help. I wondered how many department chairmen in medical schools around the world had received similar letters, and what their responses had been. So enormous was the catastrophe it left one paralyzed to act. It was like watching the parade of disasters on the 11 o'clock news and being horrified but also rendered helpless to do anything except be shocked. The distance of these horrible events from our living rooms gives them an air of unreality, which is somewhat reassuring, even though we are not proud to admit it.

In this instance, however, the letter came very close to home. The process it described was, although more extreme, very similar to what we were seeing in some of the communities in the South Bronx. Estimated HIV infection levels of up to 5 percent in the general, young adult population in severely impacted neighborhoods of the Bronx were not greatly different from what had been described in parts of central Africa. The projections of tens of thousands of AIDS-orphaned children in New York City before the end of the 1990s also bespoke a phenomenon comparable to what was being described, with rightful horror, from the front lines of the epidemic in Uganda.

In some respects, the epidemic in the South Bronx *was* as distant from the living rooms of mainstream America—whatever that was—as the AIDS-ravaged fishing villages of rural Uganda. In other respects, that distance was only increased by all the ways in which fear, denial, and prejudice continued to create a public perception of AIDS as something that affects only "other" kinds of people. It is still both unconscionable and incomprehensible to me that an epidemic of such sweeping dimensions was able to spread through poor, vulnerable inner-city communities—first in secret, then abetted by lack of interest at the highest levels of government—during the glory years of the Reagan era. Sometimes during those years, especially if I was walking around midtown Manhattan or eating in a restaurant downtown, it was possible for a moment not to be reminded of the pervasive presence of the epidemic. Back in the Bronx, reality was more intrusive, more constant.

In 1985 we started HIV antibody testing among patients in the methadone program, as part of a CDC-funded research study. At that time, the HIV antibody test had only recently been developed and was not yet available in clinical practice. The only way to be tested was through a research study such as the one we implemented in collaboration with our colleagues at CDC.

By this time, almost everyone in the 950-patient program already knew or had used drugs with someone who had died from AIDS or was sick from AIDS. We were overwhelmed by the level of interest and enthusiasm our patients showed for this study. Even though there was no treatment available at that time, most patients wanted to find out whether they had been exposed to this virus or not. Contrary to stereotype, these drug-addicted patients were concerned enough about their own health and the health of the people they loved that they were eager to have the antibody test done.

Once we started enrolling patients in the study, we could hardly keep up. I remember waking up in a cold sweat one night after the first several hundred serum samples had been sent off by Federal Express to CDC for testing, imagining what would happen if all the patients in the program turned out to be infected. How would we cope, I anguished, what would we do if they started jumping off subway platforms, overdosing indiscriminately, going on drug binges, purposely infecting past partners? The dire possibilities seemed endless.

Soon the test results started to come back, and within a few months most of the patients in the program had been identified as either positive or negative. We reassured patients, "We don't know the meaning of a positive test . . ." —which was true at the time. But we mentally assigned patients to two groups: those who had somehow managed to escape the plague and those who had not.

As it turned out, it was not 100 percent but closer to 45 percent of the patient population that was infected—still a substantial number, but not everybody. My nightmares proved unfounded: the great majority of patients who tested positive received the bad news without going berserk or bottoming out. Many considered it a "wake-up call" and took the opportunity to reflect on the meaning of their lives and try to make some constructive changes.

It was eerie not being able to predict who was positive and who was negative. In our epidemiologic studies, when we analyzed data from the entire population, it was possible to determine some behavioral risk factors for HIV infection, including the frequency of needle sharing and the use of drugs in shooting galleries. These findings were soon written up and published in medical journals, contributing to the growing literature on the epidemiology of AIDS in drug users. In individual cases, however, these risk factors were not completely predictive of patients' antibody status. It was often surprising to find that some people who had not shot up in years were positive, whereas others who were actively using were not. The rules did not appear to be absolute, and this hint of arbitrariness, of caprice, made the virus seem that much more cruel, as though mocking us.

Every month, we received our blood test results from CDC, neat computer printouts with long rows of numbers. Each row was headed by the patient's study number, followed by the date and the coded antibody test results. Our staff would then begin the process of matching these study numbers back to the names of the patients to whom they belonged, for the blood samples were sent to CDC marked only with that numerical code. In a macabre lottery, we went down the list of multiple digit numbers. When we found a study number with a positive test result next to it, we would match each digit of the six-digit number, carefully narrowing down the possible choices until finally there was only one individual to whom this unlucky prize could belong.

Holding this information, this power, and calmly classifying people in this way, I often thought of Joseph Mengele standing at the end of the train arrival platform at Auschwitz. With a flick of his cane, he summarily separated people into the saved and the damned—and in that case, as in ours, being saved was often only a provisional status. The difference, of course, was that he made these coldhearted decisions himself: we simply translated the test results from numbers to names, like grim, punctilious bookkeepers, somberly making entries in the great book of life.

Informing patients of their HIV antibody test results rapidly accustomed us to being the bearers of bad news. This process can take a heavy toll on the messenger. Sometimes, inexplicably, I would feel guilty, as if giving patients this dreaded information somehow made me responsible for it, as if it had been my fault, something that I should have been able to prevent.

Having such terrible life-and-death knowledge, being able to predict, in effect, who would live and who would die, made me feel at once both powerful and helpless. On one hand, we were able to predict people's fate in an unprecedented way; on the other, we were unable to do anything to change the inexorable sequence of events that followed.

It was particularly difficult for us, as the keepers of such ominous news, when patients chose not to receive their test results even after having consented to the test in the first place. In those days, it often took several weeks for test results to come back from CDC. For many patients, the act of having had their blood drawn enabled them to construct a fantasy of "no news is good news": if we didn't force them to return for their results—which, ethically, we felt we could not do, though we made every effort to inform them—then they must be negative. Having the information that someone was positive but not being able to share it with them made this knowledge even more burdensome. It was as if the patients had taken all of the anxiety, fear, and guilt associated with the infection and shifted it onto us, a load that many of us, with our martyrlike tendencies, were only too willing to shoulder. I had my own reasons for feeling guilty and helpless, responsible for something that in reality was not my responsibility—reasons that had to do with my father's sudden death when I was an infant—but I did not become aware of these until several years later.

Some of the most poignant dilemmas in HIV testing and counseling involved pregnancy and childbearing. It was as if the shadow of death, embodied in the virus, made the yearning for life—or the yearning to create life—that much stronger. The dilemma was that the risk of perinatal transmission of HIV could, sometimes, transform the very act of giving birth into the act of transmitting death. To complicate things still further, we knew that not all pregnant women would transmit the virus to their infants, but we had no way of predicting who would and who would not pass on the infection.

Part of what made working with pregnant women so compelling was the fact that these years coincided with my own wife Nancy's pregnancies and the birth of our two children. During this time I felt a special bond with my patients during their pregnancies, the milestones in their progress coinciding so closely with Nancy's experiences: first-trimester discomforts and how to get through them, gaining weight and not being able to fit into regular clothes, feeling the baby move, hearing the heartbeat for the first time, anticipating labor and all the potential disasters that could occur. Like a novice pilot preparing to land a plane, going through the landing sequence over and over in anticipation, then the joyful, paroxysmal moment of birth, and finally, feeling the sweet exhausted relief of seeing a healthy newborn baby for the first time.

In ways that I could do little to control, my family's path and that of my pregnant patients diverged, sometimes before and especially after the infants' birth. Most of the women I cared for faced the challenges of single parenthood, poverty, and tenuous or unsafe living conditions for themselves and their babies. When I came home and was reminded of the protective shield of safety and support that surrounded our children, I knew that this shield was something that many of my patients—not lacking in love or parenting ability—were not able to provide consistently for their children.

For the patients who were HIV infected, the contrasts were even more stark: some women began to experience a gradual physical and mental deterioration that rendered them less and less able to care for their infants. This inevitably meant that the family unit, in whatever constellation it had existed, fell apart. Aunts and grandmothers became caregivers to these dying young women and often took care of the children as well.

Children who were not infected faced the almost inevitable prospects of losing their parents, and of learning about the mixed blessings of survivorship. For children who were infected, I often witnessed a grim reversal of the normal developmental milestones of early childhood: most of these children were asymptomatic during their first six to nine months, and the mothers would bring them proudly to their follow-up visits as the children held up their heads for the first time, rolled over, sat up, and, in some cases, stood. Then, as if one were watching a video that had suddenly been switched into reverse, the children became sicker with HIV disease. They began to lose weight, and the ability to stand or sit, reverting in effect to the earlier stages of infancy through which they had just passed. This was the most painful part of it all for me. I saw my own children thrive and flourish, then witnessed these others, most of whom I had first encountered in utero as one of those insistent, staccato, fetal heartbeats, fall behind, dwindle, and die.

It is not difficult to imagine, especially in retrospect, how working in this environment for several years could lead to intense personal involvement, reduced emotional distance, and blurred boundaries between patient and physician. The distance that had existed between me and my patients during medical school and residency quickly evaporated as I was surrounded by other young adults whose lives seemed so intimately familiar to me. This sense of immediacy and identification can be a powerful source of validation and self-worth, but it can also lead—as it did in my case—to a loss of perspective, a failure to set limits, and an increasingly heavy burden for the care provider.

Some of the infants I followed shared birth dates with my own two children, and when I saw one of these kids in the clinic, I felt deeply connected; when one started to fail, I experienced a sick, vulnerable feeling as I rushed home to check on the girls, inhale their sweet baby smells, and assure myself that they were all right. I used to have a ritual every day upon coming home, which included taking off my shoes at the door, quickly changing into my "home clothes," and washing my face and hands, as if in some symbolic way I sought to create a protective boundary between the world of my family and that of my patients with AIDS in the Bronx.

Sometimes this concern had a basis in reality—when I had been exposed to patients with tuberculosis before they had been diagnosed, for example, or after sustaining an accidental needle stick and becoming convinced that I had been infected with HIV. In these situations, afraid that I had myself become the dreaded carrier of disease, I searched desperately for a way to reassure myself that I could set up a barrier to keep these plagues from my family. This need to set limits might not have been so great had the lack of boundaries not seemed so threatening to begin with.

Looking back, it is hard to appreciate how I could have failed to see that the losses and challenges facing these young parents and children might resonate with something in my own life. Dying patients, vulnerable children, families being devastated by untimely and unnatural deaths: these were all themes that defined my own experience, whether I was conscious of it or not. My first experiences with my pregnant patients and their families should have been an inkling to me that AIDS and my involvement in the epidemic were about myself and my own family in very immediate ways; yet like most sweeping realizations that profoundly change one's perspective on oneself and the world, this one had to build slowly, until it finally burst into consciousness.

Everyone I know who has worked with AIDS patients has had to face his or her own fears of becoming infected with HIV. For some, rationality prevails, while others find solace in denial or magical thinking ("I am doing God's work; I must be protected.") Others live with an ever-present fear that they have been or will become infected. In fact, most people, including myself, respond in all of these different ways, sometimes vacillating from moment to moment between feelings of vulnerability and omnipotence.

In medical school I frequently developed psychosomatic symptoms suggestive of the various diseases we were studying—Nancy used to joke that I was the only person in the world who had been afflicted by so many fatal diseases and recovered from all of them—but I would not describe myself as particularly paranoid concerning exposure to illness from patients. Once I started taking care of AIDS patients, however, I began to become more concerned about my own safety. (This followed the initial year or two of innocence before AIDS was suspected of being a blood-borne disease. Indeed, a friend of mine who was an intern in an internal medicine residency training program in Manhattan in 1982 recalls literally being laughed out of the office of a senior attending physician in infectious diseases when she protested that interns might be putting themselves at risk by having to draw so many blood samples from the patients with AIDS.)

Part of my new level of concern about AIDS had to do with the frightening newness of the disease, its uncontrolled fury, and the very real possibility of becoming infected through a needle stick or other blood exposure. But the fear of becoming infected also had to do with the lack of boundaries between myself and my patients. Seeing someone my own age, whose children shared birth dates with my own, and watching her whole life unravel before my eyes made the selectivity of the virus seem so arbitrary: "Why not me, why not my wife, why not my children?" I would ask myself. As I sat next to patients, talking to them, examining them, my hands touching their skin, I wondered where is the boundary, where is the barrier, where do they stop and I start? Sometimes I felt a kind of sad amazement as I examined a patient, knowing that just beneath the surface of the skin, in untold numbers of lymph nodes and microscopic blood vessels, the virus was multiplying, circulating quietly, efficiently, explosively.

It seemed absurd that mere skin could contain such a powerful force of nature.

In a ritual I shared with many of my colleagues—if we knew each other well enough, we sometimes talked about it—I regularly checked myself for swollen lymph nodes, Kaposi's sarcoma, shingles, or, in fleeting glances at the mirror to inspect my throat, oral thrush. If I developed symptoms of an upper respiratory infection or bronchitis, my first thought was whether this could be *Pneumocystis carinii* pneumonia or tuberculosis. If I had a fever I worried about disseminated *mycobacterium avium* or cytomegalovirus infection (both last-stage AIDS complications), and if I lost five or ten pounds due to an intermittently successful regimen of diet and exercise, I wondered whether I should credit HIV-related wasting syndrome. In fact, sometimes when I gained weight due to junk food binging around a grant or conference deadline—Genoa salami, Doritos, and Hostess chocolate donuts were my favorite forms of instant gratification—I would be secretly relieved that I was getting a little too chunky to have HIV.

These morbid preoccupations came and went, becoming more prominent in periods of high stress or anxiety. In retrospect, these concerns about illness may have served as a surrogate for some of the more wide-ranging fears that I may not have been aware of. Fear of dying, but even more, fear of abandoning my children, the projected fear of not being able to protect them from the sudden loss of their father or the devastation of the epidemic: these feelings were deep, primal terrors, flowing like an underground river through my life, originating in my own abandonment as an infant by my father. The moment he fell out of that window, the world became for me a place that was not safe, a place where bad things could happen in an instant, without warning.

My brooding daydreams about getting AIDS came into sharp focus in the fall of 1985, when I suffered a needle-stick accident after placing a tuberculin skin test on one of my pregnant HIV-infected patients. As needle sticks go, this was not as high risk as a deep injection into muscle with a blood-filled, large-bore needle, but it was still a significant exposure, particularly because the syringe did have a small amount of the patient's blood visible in it. My immediate reaction was to freeze, not believing what I had done as I felt the needle enter my index finger. Like most needle-stick accidents, this was a recapping injury: I missed while aiming the needle shaft back into the sheath. When I saw the telltale drops of my own blood, I had to suppress screaming out in horror with the patient still sitting in front of me. I still do not know whether she even noticed that I had stuck myself, but I quickly finished speaking with her and ran to the clinic bathroom, where I scrubbed my finger with soap and scalding hot water and wiped it repeatedly with alcohol. As I was doing this I recalled stories that I had heard in the Cub Scouts of mountaineers who had to amputate their own hands after snake bites to avoid having the deadly venom spread through their bodies, and I wondered whether that was what it would take for me to save myself. I kept wishing desperately that I could turn back the clock, even just five minutes, that I could get another chance to avoid sticking myself. The whole event seemed to have happened so quickly that I could almost convince myself that it had never happened at all.

I left the clinic, drove in a daze through the South Bronx back to my office at the hospital, went into my office, shut the door, and cried. I called Nancy, who was reassuring but also concerned. I didn't know who to turn to. I knew that I needed my blood drawn immediately for the baseline HIV test to document my status at the time of the exposure, so I went to one of our clinic offices near the hospital and drew the blood myself. It was an early-morning clinic, most of the staff had already left, and I made up an excuse to the security guard that I needed to go over some charts in the medical office. It was the first time that I had ever drawn blood from myself—I was too shaken and panicked to speak to anyone else at work about it—and as I sat there with the tourniquet on my arm, holding the needle in the vein, worried that someone would come in and find me, I thought how much I looked like an IV drug user hitting himself for the first time, alone, in secret. In accordance with the system that was then in place through the New York City Health Department, I labeled my blood tube with a specimen number and left it at the hospital hematology lab to be brought by courier to the City Health Department for confidential testing, knowing that it would take several weeks for the result to come back.

My thoughts still racing, I decided to leave early and drive home, and on the way there I was suddenly filled with the incredibly powerful urge to make love to my wife and father another child. This was the last thing in the world that I would ever have anticipated at such a time, but it was such a strong feeling that I suddenly and completely understood all my HIV-infected pregnant patients who chose not to terminate their pregnancies. I had a mental image of a forest fire advancing as I ran to escape its leading edge, trying to preserve something living and green, afraid I would be overtaken before I could reach sanctuary. I envisioned my body becoming diseased and held out this hope of having another child before it was too late—or before the all-consuming fire got to me—as a symbolic way of having the last word against death.

Both Nancy and I knew—even though the risk of transmission of HIV during acute infection was not as fully understood then as it is now—that there was a potential risk that she herself might become infected if I had already been exposed to the virus and we had sex. But this awareness was sufficiently dulled by denial, wishful thinking, and the intense desire to beat the virus that we went ahead anyway. (Having experienced this, it is humbling for me to consider the challenges faced by AIDS prevention programs worldwide when dealing with such elemental forces as human sexuality and reproduction.) Our second daughter, Casey, was conceived during the next several weeks.

Meantime, I even went so far as to store some semen samples at a sperm bank in Manhattan, which did not seem to me absurd or inappropriate at the time, thinking that I might preserve some "pure" specimens before the disease got to me. This, too, felt like a victory. My first antibody test, from the day of the accident, was negative, but during the four months while I was awaiting my follow-up test, I experienced all of the classic stages of grief elaborated by Elisabeth Kübler-Ross in her studies with dying patients: denial, anger, bargaining, depression, and acceptance. By the end of that time, I had come to believe that even if I was infected, I could handle it and get on with my life. Indeed, the clarity of my dialogue with myself led me to reexamine some basic priorities in my life. I came to realize, even more clearly than before, the importance of love, happiness, acceptance, and trust. When I finally got the negative result back for the follow-up test, I was profoundly relieved, but also grateful that I had gone through this process and come out the other side.

(I continued to get bills from the sperm bank for several years for the yearly storage costs of my samples. Finally I decided that I could let this go without feeling like I had jettisoned my life preserver. Several years later that institution was closed after revelations that its personnel had on more than one occasion mislabeled semen samples for artificial insemination and that women had as a result been inseminated with the wrong donor sperm. It made me wonder what the final disposition of my samples truly was.)

There was something about the intensity of the epidemic that encouraged excesses. The staff of our clinical and research program quickly came to experience our work as more than a routine, nine-to-five job. Everything had an urgency to it, a sense of having to get things done in the face of ever-impending calamity. Nothing was ever routine, crisis was perpetual. This type of environment draws some people to it just as surely as it repels others. In my case, being on the edge, living amid chaos, responding to ever-present crises was all compelling. Although I eventually learned that this frenetic pace distracted me from what was really going on inside—unresolved issues that ultimately led back to my father's death—there was something deeply gratifying about always feeling like I was trying keep a firm hold on the tiller in the midst of the storm.

This environment did not lend itself to moderation. With the half-joking refrain of, "Hey, it's an epidemic!" we routinely went without sleep, feverishly assimilated every new bit of information about AIDS, gorged ourselves on junk food, hunted patients down on street corners for follow-up, stayed up all night writing papers or grant proposals, drank too much coffee, smoked too many cigarettes. (The culture of the methadone program at the time seemed to value cigarette smoking as an alternative to heroin use, and this served, oddly, to unite patients and staff.) After a grant or conference deadline, we would sometimes have frantic, spontaneous parties, drinking alcohol in paroxysmal bursts, like a college binge after final exams.

I recognize now that I lived more on the edge than was good for me during those years, living in some respects by Nietzsche's dictum, "Whatever doesn't kill me makes me stronger." These behaviors were abetted by an unconscious belief in my own indestructibility. Now I crave sleep and look forward to being able to rest, but then to go to sleep meant to give in, to be defeated. For years I would stay up all night on a regular basis—even when I was no longer on call—to read journals, write manuscripts, plan new studies, or just catch up on paperwork. At times I actually looked forward to Nancy and the girls going to sleep so I could be alone with my work-related obsessions. Like my friends at Federal Express, whose dispatchers rely on the lightly trafficked night sky to give them the freedom they need for routing their planes—always needing to ship serum specimens or meet grant deadlines, we knew the closing hours of every Fed Ex office in the city—I saw the night as a blank canvas, a time when I could be by myself, without interruption, untouchable. To stay awake meant to stay alive, to be in control of the uncontrollable.

Music represented an important release from the daily toll of the epidemic. Some of us would drive down after work or on weekends to go dancing at the Roxy—a cavernous proto–rap and breakdance emporium on 18th Street near the docks on Manhattan's West Side—to hear the pioneering deejay Afrika Bambataa, who had honed his craft on turntables at legendary parties in Bronx housing projects. Other nights we would get into the zone with Loremil Machado and his Saravia Bahia Band at S.O.B.'s (Sounds of Brazil) on Varick Street, run over to hear Chaka Khan at the Paradise Garage, or skank to Dennis Brown and Yellowman in the smoke-filled Reggae Lounge off Canal.

The music got inside us in a way that transported us, trancelike; hypnotic, sensual, seductive, the thumping beat of the bass felt as if it were filling us with the power of life itself. Like the mythical dance against death, this was our defiance, our escape from the devastation that we faced every day. It felt good, even if it was only a brief sojourn from the pain. In many ways, it was important to have this kind of escape. The excesses became more of a problem when the behavior was not merely a healthy release but a way of covering up the pain, of not feeling the feelings that were constantly being triggered by the work.

The stretching of limits was not only personal but professional. Soon I found myself becoming one of a handful of sought-after experts on AIDS and injection drug use. By 1986 I was receiving a growing number of invitations to give talks, present papers, and participate in a variety of conferences and on advisory committees. Sometimes I felt like an impostor, an interloper. Sometimes I basked in my newfound celebrity.

I can see now how unbalanced I was during those years—how unconscious I was, on this high-profile fast lane, of my own unfinished business, of my own psychic and emotional needs. At the same time, I can still take pride in what I was able to accomplish during those years, a time of intensity and newness that will probably be unmatched in my career. The epidemic was fresh, everything was wide open, and we were at the heart of it.

Feeling literally like I had something inside me that I had to get out—a story that I had to tell—I wrote or cowrote more than thirty scientific articles, reviews, and book chapters over the course of less than five years, almost all of them on topics pertaining to AIDS and drug abuse. I had suddenly become an expert in a field that was still in its infancy, that was vast and largely unexplored.

The fact that so little was known fueled our feverish sense of urgency as we tried to describe and make sense of the epidemic that was unfolding around us. These were times for broad strokes, not for nuances, times for exploring the fundamental dynamics of the epidemic. Our studies helped define the unique characteristics of AIDS among drug users—in particular, drug users' risk factors for HIV infection and the importance of tuberculosis and bacterial infections as major sources of morbidity and mortality in this group. Our work also helped to generate early data on AIDS and pregnancy, and on transmission of HIV from mothers to infants.

As our work became better known, I began to receive an increasing number of requests to travel. More often than not, I jumped at the chance, eager to meet new people, discover new places, and play the part of visiting expert. I remember a television commercial for American Express at the time, which aptly characterized my view of myself in the world. In it, a youthful, slightly rumpled journalist is first seen through the glass of a red-painted London telephone booth, saying into the receiver, "Bangkok? Tomorrow?" Then, as the camera zooms in, he reaches into the pocket of his flannel shirt, takes out his Amex card, looks at it, smiles, and says, "Sure, no problem!"

There was something very gratifying about having my work recognized, but also something that promoted its own kind of escapism. In the same way that my patients' exaggerated expectations of me reinforced my fantasies of omnipotence, so too did these far-flung requests for my expertise inflate my sense of importance. No doubt I *did* have something worthwhile to say, and I *was* justifiably proud of our studies, which were helping to describe the special characteristics of AIDS in drug-using populations. But through all these lectures and conferences and all the papers and book chapters that I wrote during that period, I never spoke or wrote one word about the underlying personal and emotional issues that in many respects, unconsciously, defined the framework of all my other endeavors. Unbeknownst to me, my own history, my own unfinished business, was writing the script of my fast-paced wanderings in those years. Being away—working late, staying up all night writing grant proposals or papers, going club hopping in the Village, or leaving for Europe on a few days notice—all these represented different ways of *not* being present. These were ways of *not* being there for my family and my wife, ways of defending myself from intimacy in a world where life seemed so fragile, where even good people died or disappeared and there was nothing you could do to stop it. These were ways of *not* facing the central, unresolved issue in my life, the early death of my father and my own entry into fatherhood.

I had to travel hundreds of thousands of miles before I became aware of the ways in which I had been running away from home.

As I was drawn deeper into the epidemic, I found myself facing problems that I felt totally unprepared for as a physician. I had entered medical school and had been trained in a medical worldview that did not include a fatal, untreatable illness affecting large numbers of young adults and their children. The analytic processes that I had become familiar with, the medications whose uses, benefits, and side effects I had learned—indeed, the entire approach to care that I had inherited—all seemed inconsequential against this new and frightening challenge.

Paradoxically, however, something unexpected happened: AIDS, by stripping away much of the facade of what physicians were accustomed to doing with their patients, in fact brought me closer to the traditional role of the physician. In those years, before the symbolic introduction in 1987 of AZT, which rendered AIDS "treatable" (even though not very effectively at first), we empathized intensely with our patients, knowing that all that we could do for them was to be there, to promise not to abandon them, to accompany them through their illness, and to witness and relieve their suffering. The disease humbled us, it made much of our carefully accumulated medical knowledge seem irrelevant. Yet by humbling us, it deepened our solidarity with our patients.

I had not experienced such a clear connection to my patients until I was faced with this illness that I could not treat. I learned then that this role—that of an engaged witness, accompanying and helping patients through their illness—fundamentally defined my greatest usefulness as a physician, not only with patients who were deemed incurable but with all patients. For myself and our small medical group, what enabled us to play this role in our patients' lives was simply the fact that we refused to abandon them and that we had made this same journey with many others before, just as we would return for those who would surely follow. My earlier image of the physician as the "clerk of records" for the villagers became even stronger, for these villagers all seemed to be dying before their time, before they had had a chance to leave their final legacy. Indeed, my biggest fear, as the numbers of the dead increased, was that I would forget their names and faces, that they would be lost without a trace. I tried all the harder to keep my patients alive, and not to forget them when they died.

# 2  Connection

In remembering Gabriel, my first patient with AIDS, I had been afraid that his face and the faces of all my other patients would begin to blur together. In some respects, they have, but there are so many patients for whom something special stands out, whose particularity helps to protect them from facelessness.

There was an earnestness, an intensity about my drug-using patients that heightens the vividness of their memories. One of the first things I realized after starting to work with the large population of drug addicts in the methadone program was that things were never boring. I found my patients, for the most part, to be highly intelligent, adaptive, resourceful, and engaging. They were also often manipulative, sociopathic, and sometimes self-destructive, but to have survived the Darwinian struggle of life on the street to the venerable addict's age of thirty or thirty-five they had been preselected by the time I met them to be at least somewhat successful in their lifestyle. Their less adept contemporaries would have long since died either from drug overdoses or violence, or else might have left the drug-using subculture through prolonged incarceration or eventual sobriety.

There was something about these patients that reached me, that got under my skin. Some of it may have been their own lack of boundaries and their readiness to perceive me as the good parent, distinct from all the bad parents in their lives. Some of it may have been my own willingness to be perceived in this light, my own unfulfilled need to be an all-powerful rescuer. Perhaps, as I once heard it described by a visiting spiritual luminary, it was the earnest way in which drug addicts always seem to be seeking bliss but are just using the wrong means to attain it.

Many of my patients lived in constant peril, engaged in the daily battles of active drug users on the street. Some patients confided in me that this was the hardest thing to give up when they tried to stop using drugs: the feeling that every day was like an all-or-nothing roller-coaster ride, after which life's mundane realities seemed hardly worth getting out of bed for. This yearning to live intensely in every moment, on the edge, was part of what made working with this population so engrossing.

When I remember those patients who suffered and died, I also remember their persistence, their laughter, and sometimes their transcendence. More than one patient told me that getting HIV infection was in some ways a blessing in disguise: unwanted, unwelcome, but a catalyst that eventually resulted in important, conscious life changes and recovery from drug abuse. For some, AIDS remained nothing but a curse, only intensifying their self-destructiveness, until they finally died in character, alone, hateful, shrouded in fear and pain. Sometimes I had to restrain my sentimental desire for a happy ending in all cases, realizing that this did not do justice to the diversity of experience in my patients' lives: some of them would come to terms, others would take their unfinished business with them.

So many images come to mind of people and circumstances encountered in those years. The following are just a few of them:

• Martin, the fast-talking white emergency medical technician who first became addicted to Demerol as a means of self-medication for the jangled nerves he would get after all-night ambulance runs in the South Bronx. Martin was good-looking in a slightly weathered way— the image of a choirboy grown up and fallen on bad times, with a shock of wavy red-brown hair and soulful eyes—but when he smiled he had a telltale addict's mouth, a jumble of discolored, broken, and missing teeth. He came from a large Irish family in the Norwood section near Webster Avenue, which still remains a strong Irish enclave. Martin managed to get through school and become an EMT, but he developed a serious and intractable drinking problem along the way, becoming a frequent visitor to alcohol detox units in downtown Manhattan. After getting hooked on Demerol and using it for a year or two, he started shooting heroin. He became infected with HIV when, as he discovered in retrospect, he began hanging with the wrong crowd. "Luck of the draw, Pete," was how he once described it to me matter-of-factly, using a nickname I had never liked or answered to but which somehow, coming from him, seemed appropriate.

Martin often sidled up to me in the large clinic waiting room, my unsolicited confidant, offering helpful advice and suggestions: "Hey Pete, there's some bad China White out on the street, you know, it's really Fentanyl, people are OD'ing, I just thought you should know." Or "Hey Pete, you gotta help me do something about my social worker, man, this guy has got no clinical skills whatsoever." With

Martin, there was always an angle, a scam, or a scandal, which he was either in the midst of or else quick to expose with righteous indignation for whomever the guilty party was. He was quick-witted and stubborn, persevering with ironic good humor through one catastrophe after another. He used to joke that he was trying the alcohol cure for HIV, in the hope that the virus was susceptible to Irish whiskey. Martin sometimes seemed to be surviving more on stubbornness and irascibility than anything else, and when he finally died at thirty-nine, he had surprised even himself by his longevity.

• Cynthia, the petite black woman with a thick southern accent and disarming graciousness, who regularly made the rounds of the "pill doctors" off the Grand Concourse. These were street-level apartments with reinforced doors and metal grates outside and bullet-proof plexiglass windows inside, where long lines of patients would wait out on the sidewalk early in the morning, then move through with smooth efficiency to receive prescriptions through the window for "thirty, thirty, and thirty," meaning thirty pills each of Percocet, Valium, and Darvon, a quasi-legal operation that seemed to flourish, like many other scams, on the edges of the Medicaid system.

Once, over a period of four to five months, we noticed that Cynthia was becoming progressively more anemic, based on the dropping hematocrit values in her periodic blood counts. We thought at first that this might be due to a medication effect, and all of her medications were held. Her anemia continued to worsen, although it had a very odd waxing and waning pattern.

Eventually we sent her to the emergency room for a transfusion. When she arrived in the ER, I got a call from the physician there, who asked whether I knew that Cynthia had been there for transfusions four times within the two previous months. I was shocked to discover this, although it did explain in part the up-and-down patterns of her recent blood counts. When I next saw Cynthia in the clinic, I confronted her and she admitted, shyly, that she had gotten involved in yet another Medicaid scam: this one involved a storefront office around the corner from our clinic, where patients would give blood samples at the rate of $10 for ten tubes of blood. (In the currency of the street, this was worth two vials of crack.) The so-called laboratory would then bill Medicaid and be reimbursed for tests that were not performed. Cynthia admitted that she had engaged in this practice more than twenty times and had periodically gone to the emergency room to get a transfusion—also billed to Medicaid—when she became too weak and short of breath to go on.

This was the same Cynthia who, with complete sincerity, could come to see me in the clinic and ask for a refill of her Percocet prescription that she said had been snatched off her night table by a little bird that had flown in her window. She also managed, in a way that seemed to defy gravity, to be able to hold herself at a sustained forty-five-degree angle to the horizontal when she was nodding on pills, as if she were being supported by an invisible strut. If you roused her with a loud noise she would pick up her head, startled, and then straighten herself, smiling demurely.

She made a heroic effort to stop taking pills when she became pregnant, especially when she found out, after an amniocentesis (she was already in her early forties), that the sixteen-week fetus was a female. She promptly named it Cynthia and came dutifully to all her prenatal appointments, keeping a detailed chart of her weight gain and the baby's growth. She became convinced that this baby was her last chance to get her life together and be successful at something. At twenty-four weeks she began having vaginal bleeding and went into premature labor on the subway in lower Manhattan. Cynthia was taken to Bellevue Hospital, where doctors were unable to stop her labor: the baby weighed less than 1000 grams at delivery and died of a brain hemorrhage after a couple of weeks in the neonatal intensive care unit. When I next saw Cynthia she was in a pill-head haze, mumbling to herself as she sat in the waiting room, head slumped over. She was arrested not long after that—for what I don't know—and was sent up to Bedford Hills, a women's state prison, for a couple of years. I kept expecting her to resurface somewhere, but I never saw her again.

• Marta, the twenty-four-year-old who came to New York with her family from Puerto Rico at the age of five and then grew up too quickly on the streets of the lower East Side. She had left home when she was fourteen and had since lived by her wits on the street and in juvenile institutions. Marta was under five feet tall, boyish-looking, with crackling, nervous energy, and—like many of my female patients—had an array of short scars across both forearms, stigmata of adolescent suicide attempts (gestures, too often unheeded). She was an affecting mixture of toughness and vulnerability, as she busily set up barriers and defenses while desperately longing for someone to break through them. She had wild, spiky hair, was covered with tattoos, and had countless rings and studded bracelets, numerous pierced body parts, motorcycle boots, and various layers of leather.

Marta came to see me for prenatal visits with her boyfriend, Buck, a toothless tattoo artist, similarly festooned; Buck was the one person in her life who she ever felt had loved her, and he dutifully accompanied her to all her appointments.

During these prenatal visits, Marta often reminded me of a female medieval knight coming in with Buck, her loyal squire. As she carefully removed her ornaments and protective paraphernalia, Buck stood beside her, gathering them up in his arms. As her armor came off, her scowling features relaxed, and she became almost childlike in her anticipation. Then the two of them held hands together in awe as Marta lay on the examining table and they listened to the sound of the baby's heartbeat with the fetal stethoscope. When the static of the microphone suddenly gave way to the insistent pulsing of the fetal heart, they giggled together. One day as I watched them, it occurred to me that if there was an image of "The American Family" for the Bronx, 1986, this was it.

• Hector, a fiery-eyed Puerto Rican man in his forties who had been doing well in treatment but who came in one day complaining of severe itching and the belief that thousands of little white bugs had crawled under his skin, a common symptom among heavy crack users. After first checking his skin—I had learned it was always important to try to substantiate or disprove even the most bizarre-sounding scenarios—and determining that there was no evidence of such an infestation, I reassured him that this was most likely an effect of the drug. He remained unconvinced and suddenly started scratching his head frantically, pulling out small clumps of hair. He thrust one of these clumps of hair in my face, and with a wild cackle that sounded like an old backwoods prospector who had just struck gold, pointed excitedly to the little white follicles at the end of each strand of hair, exclaiming, "You see, look at them crawling, they're in my head!" Realizing what was the source of his confusion, I pulled out a couple of strands of my own hair to show him that these imagined bugs were no more than the normal ends of the hair shaft. He screamed and jerked back, looking at me wildly, crying out, "Oh my God, Doc, you have them too!"

Hector always looked at me a little askance after that episode, convinced, I am certain, that I suffered from the same affliction that so tormented him. A few months later, he told me he was moving back to Puerto Rico (his HIV disease had progressed, and he did not want to die in New York, plus he had a friend outside San Juan who was going to get him to distribute some righteous "rock" cocaine); a year later, word filtered back that he had died of a drug overdose. I always suspected that it was intentional: he had once told me he would overdose

on pure *manteca*—Spanish for lard, Puerto Rican street slang for
heroin—if his disease ever got so bad that he couldn't take it anymore.

• Frank, the frail white man in his fifties who had been a literary
editor for a major publishing house and who became addicted to
heroin as a form of self-medication for his then-undiagnosed manic-
depressive illness. He often reminded me of a less extreme William
Burroughs, urbane, seedy, gracefully deteriorating, prowling about
in a threadbare old overcoat he might once have purchased at Aber-
crombie and Fitch.

It was not until Frank had lost his job, gotten strung out on heroin,
hit bottom, become HIV infected, and entered our methadone program that finally, a decade too late, he had been diagnosed as a manic
depressive by our program psychiatrist. After being started on appropriate medications, he was able to live what he felt was a normal, well-
modulated life. He appreciated the irony of this situation and sometimes laughed about it, with a wry twinkle in his eye, observing that
he had to come close to dying in order to be able to live.

Yet I never heard him express any regret, and he remained a digni-
fied, gentle soul to the end, often playing an avuncular role for some
of our more agitated younger patients. The chasms of race and class,
always just beneath the surface in our society, would seem to be
bridged, for a moment, in the image of Frank walking down the street
with Melvin, a young black patient in our program, also HIV infected,
whom Frank was tutoring to help get his high school equivalency degree. Walking away from the clinic, Frank resting his right arm
lightly on Melvin's shoulder, the other arm gesturing broadly as he
spoke, Frank looked like a favorite uncle having just returned home
after a long absence to impart his worldly wisdom to a wide-eyed and
adoring nephew.

Frank was a wise and thoughtful man, who seemed to rise above his difficult circumstances with a poise and an elegance that were inspiring. The many patients from our program who packed the funeral home when he died—in contrast to his own family, with which he had had no contact in years—were a testament to his gentle but strong influence.

• Naida, a thirty-five-year-old Puerto Rican woman, was one of the first pregnant women in the methadone program to be tested for HIV infection. Naida looked tough on the outside—dyed flaming red hair, leather jacket, thick silver rings, tattoos, and spoke with a heavy Bronx accent—but she possessed a disarming quality of domesticity and innocence. She had an eight-year-old daughter, mentally retarded, on whom she doted. Naida had had no evidence of HIV-related disease and did not seem to be at high risk, because she hadn't injected drugs in more than four years. She had agreed to the HIV test without hesitation at her first prenatal visit.

At that first clinic visit, I felt the top of the uterus at twenty centimeters, consistent with twenty weeks' gestation, and we easily heard the strong and steady fetal heartbeat. Naida beamed as she heard it; she had not had this experience during her first pregnancy, years before. We drew blood for the standard prenatal tests, plus an additional sample to send to CDC for HIV antibody testing. Because my suspicion was so low, I did not even think to ask CDC to accelerate the normal two- to three-week turnaround for tests.

I was horrified to discover after this waiting period that Naida's test was positive. At her follow-up prenatal visit that week, she told me that she had decided not to receive her test results because she had realized that she would continue the pregnancy no matter what. This was years before the discovery that taking AZT during pregnancy could reduce the risk of transmission of HIV; indeed, it was two years before AZT had been used at all in patients with AIDS. I asked Naida whether, if she were told that her test was positive, she could imagine making a different decision, to terminate the pregnancy. She said she wasn't sure. This left me in the impossible position of knowing something that might affect her decision but being unable to tell her.

I decided that I was obliged to convey what she needed to know. Although I felt conflicted, I decided that I had to come as close as I could to telling her that her test was positive without actually saying the words. She could then choose whether or not to be confronted with what she did not want to hear. Naida's pregnancy—by this time almost twenty-three weeks—was already far past the point of an uncomplicated abortion, and indeed I knew of only one institution in New York City where she could have undergone a late-second-trimester termination even if she had wanted to. With my hand on the phone, I told her that if she thought she would change her mind after receiving her test results, then I needed to inform her of those results and make an appointment for her to be evaluated for a pregnancy termination. She looked at me, sighed, repeated that she did not want the results, and said that she wanted me to help her have a healthy baby. I smiled, took my hand off the phone, told her that of course I would help her, and we never spoke about her HIV status again.

After the baby was born, another daughter, Naida dutifully brought the baby in for checkups—including having her blood serially tested for HIV antibody—but Naida never acknowledged her own status nor sought medical care for it. She remained asymptomatic for at least another three years (after which time I lost touch with her). The baby was born healthy and remained so during the first several years of her life, although follow-up blood tests showed that she was indeed infected.

• Luis and Blanca, the young married couple who enrolled in our program after moving to the Bronx from Queens with their five small children. They seemed devoted to each other and to their family, until things began to disintegrate under the growing weight of HIV. Luis, who was more advanced than his wife in HIV disease, had a childlike, naive quality; his self-preservation instincts seemed too undeveloped for him ever to have survived as a drug user on the street. Blanca, in contrast, was more calculating and distrustful, managing the details of Luis's life in much the same way she did for her children. As he became sicker, she became more controlling, and once they left Queens, where his family still lived, he was even more dependent on her.

Abruptly, in what struck me as a last gesture of rebellion, denial, or self-indulgence, Luis had a brief affair with Wanda, a woman who lived in the same apartment building where he and Blanca had moved. Wanda—whom I met once, when she came to visit Luis in the hospital—was a shy, melancholy young woman with dark brown eyes and a surprisingly cherubic face. She had previously tested negative for HIV, and she shrugged off any concerns about acquiring the virus through sex with Luis. She loved him too much, she said, to be worried about that, and in fact not using condoms was a sign of her devotion to him. Although I counseled her about the risks, I did not at first perceive her behavior as being intentionally self-destructive. If I had, I might have anticipated what happened several months later, after Luis had broken off the affair and returned to Blanca. Wanda locked herself in her apartment, called him to come and see her, and then told him through the peephole, behind her barricaded door, that she could not live without him. She proceeded to take a fatal overdose of barbiturates, emptying in one gulp an old bottle of sleeping pills that was in her medicine cabinet. By the time 911 was called and the ambulance arrived, she was dead.

Luis's health declined quickly over the next six months, particularly after he developed CMV retinitis. This infection can progress swiftly to blindness if untreated. (Three medications are now available to suppress this infection; in Luis's time, there was no treatment available outside of an experimental research protocol in which he chose not to participate because he would have had to stop taking AZT in order to qualify.) Luis's first symptoms were blurred vision and "floaters"—the sensation of specks or small dark blotches in the field of vision—and by the time he was seen in clinic he had begun to lose sight in both his eyes.

His retinitis progressed rapidly, and within another month, Luis was completely blind, and more dependent on Blanca than ever. I visited him frequently during his hospitalization for his last illness, and he still maintained his trusting, positive outlook, always greeting me with a big smile and an outstretched hand at the sound of my voice. Even though he had willingly given up his sight in order to remain on AZT, this drug alone—as we now know—was unable to stave off the relentless advance of his disease, and he soon died.

Several months after Luis's death, Blanca left the methadone program and took her children back to Queens. Before she left, she mentioned to her drug counselor that she was thinking about getting back together with an old boyfriend there, and maybe having several more children, but I do not know if she ever did.

• Donnell, the small, wiry black man in his late thirties who had worked for years as a paralegal in a downtown law firm until crack and heroin got the better of him and he lost his job and his life savings. He came to the methadone clinic every day, impeccably dressed in a suit, hair neatly trimmed and pomaded, nails manicured and shining, and he carefully maintained his dignity and style to the end. Although I often felt as if he was scamming me, with a used car salesman's handshake and his polished, ingratiating manner, I was always happy to see him and was gratified by his eager involvement in his own medical care.

Whatever Donnell did, he approached it with the same level of burning intensity. Years before peer education was a widely accepted component of AIDS prevention, he became zealously involved in outreach efforts to help educate active drug users on the street and in shooting galleries, and he gave lectures to community groups and high school students, speaking out about the dangers of AIDS and the best ways to protect against HIV transmission. He could captivate an audience with his story, talking fast and excitedly, punctuating his narrative with nervous hand gestures as he exhorted his audience not to make the same mistakes that he had made.

I still can picture him, just after his third admission to the hospital for PCP, lying in his hospital bed, gasping for air, talking breathlessly into the phone to the registrar at Bronx Community College, where he was taking night classes to complete his college degree, explaining that he needed to take a slightly longer leave of absence than anticipated before returning to school. To hear him describe it over the phone, his life-threatening illness required only a minor change in plans. He survived that bout of pneumonia and a subsequent case of disseminated tuberculosis—which he probably contracted from another patient with TB who was a close friend—but he never made it back to school.

Donnell was one of my first patients to take AZT, in 1987. He became terribly nauseated from the drug and required frequent transfusions for anemia—a common side effect of AZT, especially with the high doses that we used at that time—but he was adamant about doing *something* to fight the virus. He said he would often lie awake at night, in the dark, imagining the virus multiplying inside of him, like a silent swarm of locusts: taking AZT gave him the opportunity, in his mind, to fight back. A year later, as he made his preparations for death, he insisted that his body should be cremated after his funeral. Even though this was not his family's tradition, he found some small solace in knowing that *he* would, finally, cause the virus to be destroyed with him.

At Donnell's funeral, an eight-by-ten framed photograph sat on top of the closed casket: suit and tie, hair styled, skin scrubbed, confident smile, his image had survived the ravages of his disease.

• Eddie, an intense thirty-four-year-old Italian from the Belmont section of the Bronx (home of Dion and the Belmonts), who was reported to have been an enforcer for some upper-echelon drug dealers in New Jersey. (When I first examined him and noticed several gunshot wound scars in his abdomen, he said offhandedly, gold-capped teeth shining, "I ran into a tight squeeze at this warehouse in Bayonne . . .") In spite of his violent history, people who knew him said that he had calmed down significantly in the previous few years—which always made me appreciate the fact that I was only a recent acquaintance.

He approached his illness with the same unflinching matter-of-factness with which he must have confronted the many other life-threatening situations he had faced: he wanted to know the odds, to make any decisions that had to be made, and then not look back. He made it clear that he wanted to stay alive long enough to help care for his wife Brenda (who was also ill with HIV-related disease) and their daughter Melissa (who was not), and then to make a quick exit with as much dignity as he could muster. Melissa was a few years older than my older daughter, and Eddie and I would often talk about the joys and challenges of being a father. I was moved by his fierce protectiveness toward his daughter, his dedication to her safety and happiness, and his sad awareness that he would not be there to watch her grow up. I was struck by the way these loving feelings toward his daughter coexisted in his heart with the cold-blooded ruthlessness that I also knew was there.

Eddie had managed, through a friend who had an inside track with a shady insurance company, to get a life insurance policy for himself even though he was HIV positive. This, as he put it, was the only reason that he had decided not to take himself out, for that would have prevented his wife from collecting on the policy. There was a coldness in Eddie's eyes that sometimes bordered on menacing; but there was also a sincerity and directness that were endearing. He did not suffer fools lightly, but was unfailingly loyal to his friends, grateful for what was done for him, and he lived consistently by his own stern code of ethics. The last time I saw him, before he became ill and died suddenly from overwhelming sepsis, he came to see me in the clinic, and had brought with him to show me a pair of virtual reality glasses and an accompanying cassette tape—a technology that had just appeared on the market. We sat next to each other, passing the glasses back and forth, calling out and shaking our heads in amazement, like sixth-grade classmates who had just discovered a peephole into the girls' locker room.

• Margaret, who was Jewish and had grown up in Mount Vernon, a modest suburb just north of the Bronx. When she was a teenager, she had gotten addicted to Valium and other pills, which she would get from her father, a doctor. From her suburban beginnings she began a descent whose milestones included dropping out of high school, running away from home, learning to shoot heroin and cocaine, and surviving on the streets of the Bronx in whatever ways she could.

She walked into the methadone program looking like the last survivor of a shipwreck, who had managed to hold onto some floating wreckage just long enough to get to dry land. She was twenty-six years old, emaciated, chalk-white, with matted, dirty hair, and hollow, sunken eyes. Her skin was covered with open sores from countless cocaine injections and the compulsive scratching common among cocaine addicts.

She told me that she wanted to get onto the methadone program because she was having trouble making it on the street and she was afraid of getting killed by one of her tricks. Margaret was one of the ragged legion of street prostitutes who worked under the Bruckner Expressway, where furtive front seat blow jobs went for five dollars

and where many of the drive-by customers were men from the sub-
urbs on their way home to wives and families. Vaginal intercourse
was a little more expensive, especially if the women agreed not to use
condoms. Margaret would sometimes do twenty tricks a night, which
was almost enough to support her drug habit. She told me that she
mostly needed the money for the coke, and she needed the "dope"
(heroin) so she would be too numb to care about the sex.

She had gotten badly beaten up the night before, and winced frequently as I examined her. When I saw her weeping sores, her
bruises, and her mouth—almost toothless, just a few brown, cracked
teeth remaining in her swollen gums—I was reminded of the raw
brutality of the street sex trade. As the father of two small girls, I also
felt horror as I saw how far into the depths this woman had fallen, this
woman who had once been a cute, bright-eyed little girl. There were
not many things in medicine that still made me queasy, but I began to
feel dizzy while examining her, as I contemplated the kind of world in
which parents could not protect their daughters from such a future.

Seeing the oral thrush in Margaret's mouth—a fungal infection
that is a sign of advanced HIV disease—I was also reminded of the
implications of Margaret's type of sex work for HIV transmission. Although some groups of commercial sex workers have promoted safer
sex practices, and though the use of condoms and other precautions is
standard in higher-priced settings, women in situations like Margaret's have always been vulnerable. (Women involved in street sex
transactions are at greater risk of acquiring HIV than of transmitting it
to their clients, but the risk clearly exists in both directions. During
the years I worked in the Bronx, I would often wonder about the faceless johns that patients like Margaret would describe to me; since then,
I have seen a number of middle-class heterosexual male patients with
HIV whose suburban lives have been shattered by their secretive for-
ays into the inner-city sex trade of the 1980s.)

Margaret entered the methadone program and did well for a while but eventually got strung out on crack again and went back to her former life on the street. She was hospitalized for pneumonia and sepsis a few times along the way, as her HIV disease advanced inexorably as well. By the time of her last illness, just after her twenty-eighth birthday, she had wasted away to eighty pounds and looked almost like a corpse in her hospital bed.

I went to see her in the hospital, and as I sat beside her in her room, I thought I heard the faint meowing of a cat. At first I dismissed it as my imagination, and then I heard it again. When I asked Margaret to explain, she hesitated, then smiled sheepishly as she slowly reached over and opened the bottom drawer of her night table. A little kitten poked its head over the side and Margaret picked it up, holding it protectively. I realized that this kitten was probably the one creature left in the world with which Margaret still had any loving connection. She had long since broken any ties with her family, and her relationships on the street were mostly predatory. Seeing her smile as she stroked the purring kitten's back, I was struck by this example of how the human heart can stay open to love despite all of the pain and indignities of the world. Of course, it was a flagrant violation of all relevant health codes to have a cat in her hospital room, but I agreed not to turn her in to the nursing staff. Unfortunately, her secret was discovered a few days later, and the kitten went to the animal shelter, where I hoped that someone would rescue it from its fate in a way that no one had ever been able to rescue its owner.

• Frankie and Magaly, a young couple—both HIV infected—with three small children under the age of five, had already lost one child to AIDS. Magaly, in a pattern that was all too common in the neighborhoods where our patients lived, had been sixteen when she started hanging around with Frankie, a handsome older man of twenty-four who introduced her to sex, drugs, and, later, HIV. By the time I met her, many years later, she had already begun to show telltale signs of HIV disease—weight loss, fatigue, thinning hair, skin rashes—yet she was heroic and selfless, willingly playing the role of the martyr in the family, long accustomed to putting up with Frankie and his excesses. Frankie, who had already been hospitalized for an AIDS-related pneumonia, was mean-spirited, cynical, and violent, although he was fiercely devoted to his children and, in his own way, to his wife.

Frankie had been moderately successful as a crack dealer, but, by his account, had been double-crossed by his friends, who set him up to get busted. He did a year in an upstate prison and came back embittered and penniless. Released under a special legal provision, frequently invoked, that permitted early release for inmates with AIDS, Frankie had deteriorated rapidly. The clinic social workers had been able to get him disability payments, which, because of an initial dispute, had resulted in a large retroactive payment of several thousand dollars once the claim was finally settled. Eager for small victories, our social work and counseling staff took justifiable pride in having helped obtain these resources for Frankie and his family.

To his credit, Frankie put away some money for the care of the kids, but he quickly went out and spent two thousand dollars from the disability award on some "blow" and a matching pair of thick, solid gold chains for him and Magaly. He looked like a wizened potentate as he was pushed into the clinic in his wheelchair, gold chains gleaming, handing out favors and advice to his friends, basking in the newfound respect he could command. His triumph, though sweet, was short-lived: over the next few months, he became steadily sicker and died.

Magaly continued bravely for several years, missing Frankie terribly but also, at times, realizing how angry she was at him for ways in which he had mistreated her. She later told me, only half in jest, "I wish that son of a bitch was still alive so I could kill him!" She did the best she could with the children, though toward the end it became painful to watch her come into the clinic every day to receive her methadone, children in tow, as she became progressively weaker. Sadly, it was clear that, given the absence of an extended family, the helpless offspring would soon be cast into the frightening maze of the foster care system. It sometimes seemed that Magaly simply willed herself to stay alive as long as she possibly could, to fend off the forces that she knew would scatter her children when she died.

I remember last seeing the children, on the occasion of our annual holiday party for the patients. They were laughing and fresh-faced as their mother bundled them up in winter jackets from the unofficial clothing exchange that we operated in the clinic. Each of them clutched a Christmas gift (the program counselors would scramble every year for donations from local toy stores and other vendors) wrapped in bright red and green wrapping paper. That was an image that I consciously sought to preserve as I saw them go out into the cold afternoon air on Jerome Avenue, imagining wistfully that this memory might help protect them from the pain and disillusionment that lay ahead.

• Carmen, a quiet, gentle Dominican woman with large doe eyes and a soft voice, who became pregnant at the age of thirty-three after having been told repeatedly that she could never conceive a child. She was brimming with excitement at her first prenatal visit, insistent on seeing her blood pregnancy test result with her own eyes so that she could be sure it was true. She was already by then in the symptomatic stages of HIV disease and felt that it was a miracle that she had finally been able to become pregnant after years of trying. In this case, we were concerned not only about transmission of HIV to the baby but about Carmen's health and ability to sustain a pregnancy. She was adamant about keeping the baby, however, saying that this was clearly a gift from God and that it was her last mission on earth to give birth to a child who would escape this scourge. Although I was

pessimistic about the prospects, her certainty was so compelling that I
could only support her wholeheartedly.

Although Carmen did have complications during the pregnancy,
she survived them and gave birth to a healthy, normal-weight, full-
term baby girl. In the delivery room, she announced that she would
name her Rebecca, and I can still see Carmen's face shining with gratitude, relief, and pride as she said this. The baby was ill several times
during the first three months of life, and we were concerned about
her HIV infection status, but her antibody tests became negative after
six months, and at one year she showed no signs of infection or illness. (At that time, there were no tests available to detect the presence
of HIV infection in newborns. The HIV antibody test, which was the
only available test for infection, was always positive at birth if the
mother was infected, because all babies carry maternal HIV antibodies
that have crossed the placenta. Parents and care providers thus sometimes endured several years of worried uncertainty, anxiously waiting to see whether the babies would revert to negative antibody status
and show no evidence of HIV disease. If so, they probably had es-
caped perinatal infection. Fortunately, with current viral assays it is
now possible to answer this question much closer to the time of
birth.)

Carmen moved to the east Bronx and left our program six months
after Rebecca was born, and I lost touch with the family and the baby.
More than five years later, while in a bookstore in lower Manhattan, I
noticed a book of photographs about people with AIDS. Looking
through this collection of glossy, handsome photos, I noticed a
child's face whose expression was vaguely familiar, and I realized that
the face reminded me of Carmen, whom I had not thought about for
years. I quickly turned back to the page and saw from the caption that
this was in fact her daughter Rebecca. The caption said that this child
had been born to a mother with HIV but was now, at age three, known

to be uninfected herself. The little girl looked as beautiful, full of life, and unscathed by death as any child has ever been. I closed the book and smiled, thinking of Carmen, realizing that she had indeed achieved her greatest desire.

Like a river that starts to swell, flowing more strongly as it is fed from thousands of little tributaries, I find that each memory, each face, each situation, recalls another one, until I experience a flood of images, recollections, and connections. Through all of these recollections, I am drawn, unfailingly, to five patients who have particular meaning for me because in some way, which I was unaware of at the time, each of them touched something in me that would eventually unlock my own story and help me to find my own meaning in the epidemic.

I remember Nelson most vividly, less because we shared the same birthday than for the gentle sweetness of his soul. In our population of methadone program patients, in which the patients with the most extreme personality disorders seemed to require the most attention, Nelson stood out in his sincerity, thoughtfulness, and calm. Unlike many other patients, he had an emotional maturity that enabled him to talk about his fears, concerns, and feelings about the disease without taking refuge in further drug use or other escapes. Sometimes, working with our patient population, it was easy to become overwhelmed with this sea of neediness, and with the feeling that no matter what you did, it would never be enough. One of our physician assistants who worked at the large clinic site on Jerome Avenue used to say that, from the moment she walked in the door until she left in the evening, she felt so pulled at, so tugged at to meet all these endless emotional needs that she envisioned herself having to grow an additional seven or eight breasts to keep up with the demand for her attention. Nelson was not like that, and as a result he tended to draw staff to him in a way that made it clear that they were getting as much emotional support and positive energy from him as they were giving in return.

His wife, Marilinda, who accompanied him to all of his medical visits, was also gentle, composed, and a model of grace under pressure. Their only child, Manuel, was twelve, and it was clear that his parents had been successful thus far in protecting him from the overriding influence of the street, in their neighborhood not far from Yankee Stadium, south of the Cross-Bronx Expressway. This close-knit family of father, mother, and only child stirred something in me that I did not identify consciously at the time. It was an image of the ideal family that I had never experienced, or had experienced only too briefly before it was erased from my memory.

Nelson was the first patient for whom I wrote a prescription for AZT, the first week that the drug became available, in spring 1987. I remember carefully writing the words on the prescription, foreseeing that this would be the first of thousands of such prescriptions that I would write. Nelson and I had both been anticipating the arrival of AZT on the market, and indeed for everyone involved in the epidemic at the time this was a momentous event: it represented, for the first time, the possibility that this virus could be treated. Everything that we had done up to then was supportive care. With the advent of AZT, we were at last fighting back at the virus itself, however crudely or ineffectively.

Both of us knew, at the moment I handed him the prescription, that this would probably not be enough to keep him alive much longer, that this was probably going to be, for him, too little too late. Yet for both of us, at that same moment, AIDS suddenly lost a little bit of its terror and mystery.

I took the train that day to Washington, D.C., to attend the Third International Conference on AIDS at the Washington Hilton. I arrived in time to see District of Columbia police arresting demonstrators who were picketing outside the hotel to protest the federal government's inaction on AIDS, while a flustered Vice President George Bush tried to address the audience inside over the interruptions of hecklers from the AIDS activist group Act Up. He seemed perplexed, as if he didn't understand what all the fuss was about, and before leaving was heard to mutter to an associate, with the microphone still on, something to the effect of, "What is this, a gay group or something?" How far removed this world of Washington politics was from the daily lives and struggles of my patients back home.

That year, like every year before and since that I have gone to the International AIDS Conferences, I had left with a hopeful send-off from my patients—"Hey, Doc, bring us back the cure!"—only to return empty handed: better informed, more up-to-date, but without The Cure. I fantasized that one year we would all arrive and, like troops being addressed by their victorious general at the end of a war, we would be met by some high-level scientific dignitary, who would tell us that they now had a cure, would thank us for our work, and then dismiss us to go back to our lives and families. So far, this hasn't happened, and I don't expect that it will. (There was much enthusiasm about the prospects of potent new therapies expressed nine years later at the XI International Conference on AIDS in Vancouver in 1996, and at every major AIDS conference since then, yet these new findings have only underscored the difficulties involved in translating these discoveries into real-life benefits for many of our patients. Although the advances in treatment are indeed remarkable and welcome, issues of cost, unequal access to medical care, poverty, drug addiction, adherence to complicated and demanding medication schedules, lifelong therapy with multiple medications—often adding up to more than twenty pills per day—and significant drug toxicities, all continue to pose formidable barriers to the effective use of these rigorous new therapies in many affected populations. I am reminded, bitterly, that even if a simple cure were found for AIDS, which is highly unlikely, this would not necessarily amount to an end to the epidemic. Witness the history of syphilis, for which simple curative therapy—a single shot of penicillin in many cases—has been available for nearly fifty years but which remains a significant health problem in many parts of the world, including some communities in the United States.)

After doing well on AZT for about six months, Nelson started to fail, first losing weight, then starting to lose his balance and coordination, and then becoming more apathetic and withdrawn. One day, he had a seizure in the clinic and was rushed to the North Central Bronx Hospital emergency room, where a CAT scan revealed a large circular lesion in one of the frontal lobes of his brain. This was likely either cerebral toxoplasmosis (a serious brain infection) or lymphoma (a form of cancer that affects the brain), but the diagnosis could be made only by performing a brain biopsy. At that time, it was virtually impossible to find surgical consultants at our hospital who were willing to perform procedures on AIDS patients, and this case was no exception. In addition, both Nelson and his wife had decided that if he were to become sick again, they would not want further aggressive treatment if the quality of his life would be unlikely to improve. We treated him empirically for a week with medication that would be effective against toxoplasmosis, if that were in fact his diagnosis, but he showed no improvement. His mental status continued to decline, and he began to slip in and out of consciousness.

The last time I saw him, I sat by his bedside and took his hand. He opened his eyes, smiled weakly, said, "Thank you for being here," and squeezed my hand briefly. Marilinda, who had been sitting nearby, began to cry softly. I talked with her a little while and then watched as she gave him a sponge bath. I had never been to a baptism, but there was something sacred about the way she washed his body with such long, methodical, and loving movements; it seemed as if she knew that this would be the last time she would touch his living body, and that she wanted to linger over it all the more. He died in his sleep that night.

A few months before his final illness, Nelson had told me that he had one unfulfilled wish: to return to Puerto Rico and ride his motorcycle again. He had an old Harley-Davidson, which he had restored from parts and kept stored in a friend's garage on the island. He giggled as he conjured up the image of himself, already beginning to look a little emaciated, racing over hills and around steep mountain bends near his family's home in the central coffee-growing region of Maricao. Not being certain that he could tolerate such a trip, but realizing that it was important for him to go regardless, we arranged for Nelson to have enough medication for several weeks, and local medical backup if he needed it. He sent me a postcard and returned several weeks later, bronzed from the sun and laughing, saying matter-of-factly that there was nothing else he had left to do. (I remember thinking at the time how wonderful it must be to have that feeling.) It was soon after that trip that he began to descend rapidly into his final illness.

I went to Nelson's funeral one rainy evening, at a small funeral parlor in East Harlem. He was lying in an open coffin in a room with red velour walls and dark wooden chairs. I approached the casket, stood and bowed my head for a moment and saw that they had a done a nice job preparing him. He was wearing a pressed dark brown suit, hair neatly combed, hands clasped in front holding a rosary. I wondered, as I always do in such situations, where he really was at the moment, and wished him well wherever he was. I turned away from the casket, saw Marilinda, gave her a hug, and then noticed his parents, whom I had briefly met in the hospital. Nelson's father, misty-eyed, pressed my hands clumsily between his and said in Spanish, "Thank you, we will never forget what you did for our son." These words, spoken to me from a father about his son, touching on death, and remembrance, and love, moved me greatly and reaffirmed for me as I walked out into the night that I had chosen the work I needed to do. I still did not realize how close to home these words would come in my own life, how much they would touch my long-dormant feelings about the loss of my father and his memory. Words from a father about his son, spoken in gratitude to another man's son who had grown up without his father. As I watched this family confront the loss of its father, husband, and son—seeing Nelson's life reflected in relation to his survivors—it stirred something in me that was both numb and painful, something which would eventually lead me back to my childhood history.

Milagros was a twenty-six-year-old Puerto Rican woman who looked much smaller than her twenty-eight weeks of pregnancy when I first met her. Hostile and suspicious, she had missed many prenatal appointments and had been told that morning by her counselor in the methadone program that she couldn't get her dose until she waited to see me.

She had a tiny frame, with dark, angry eyes, black hair, and sharply defined features. Her belly protruded, but only slightly, like a little bud that had not yet fully emerged. In spite of her obvious resentment at being forced to see me, and the years of neglect that her body had suffered, her face had a look that under other circumstances might even have been called elegant.

Milagros had grown up in Puerto Rico and had moved to New York with her mother as a teenager when her parents separated, a disruptive move that had left her vulnerable to the lure of the streets. She started using drugs, and, in a familiar pattern, became involved with an older man who promised—I was never sure whether these men actually believed this—to take care of her. She drifted further away from her mother, the man started to beat her, and she left home for good.

By the time I met Milagros, she had come to know intimately the depths of the city and the full dimensions of human cruelty and suffering; she had been to places of horror that I am sure she could never have imagined as a girl in Puerto Rico. When I first saw her, she had been in our methadone program for a year or so but was not doing well. Having become addicted to crack, she was now using large amounts of heroin to get "straight" from all the cocaine. She was supporting her drug habit through street sex work, which is how she had become pregnant. Although she was HIV infected, Milagros did not have advanced HIV disease and was at much higher immediate risk of becoming sick or dying from drug abuse than from the virus. She continued to prostitute despite her pregnancy, and she had refused to enter an inpatient cocaine treatment program, saying that she would rather die than be locked up.

More than any other patient I have known before or since, Milagros looked to me like someone who had already died, someone whose body was still going through the motions but whose hollow eyes revealed a spirit that had already moved on. Although I have since learned that people can heal and recover from even the most horrifying abuse and despair, in Milagros's case I felt that her experience had literally brought her into the realm of the dead, from which she could not return. What made this observation even more alarming was the fact that she had a baby inside which was very much alive, as evidenced by the strong, fast fetal heartbeat and active kicking movements that were plainly visible when I examined Milagros's abdomen.

It was clear to me and to the rest of the program staff that Milagros was in desperate need of inpatient drug treatment and close monitoring of her pregnancy, but she firmly and steadfastly refused all such interventions. We had prolonged debates within our group and with the hospital's lawyers and ethicists concerning our right to impose treatment versus the patient's right to refuse. The fact that Milagros was pregnant seemed to change our usual approach to patients who refused care, making us feel more obliged to intervene in this case not only on her behalf but also for the sake of the baby. It was a particularly helpless feeling to watch someone act so self-destructively and yet be powerless to stop it—this was something I had not consciously experienced before.

The consensus among our legal advisers was that unless she became overtly suicidal, we could only encourage Milagros to accept care, we could not compel her to do so—either for herself or for the baby. I could understand this position from the standpoint of patient autonomy and self-determination, and I had come to appreciate that part of honoring patients' autonomy included allowing them to make bad choices for themselves as long as they were able to understand the implications of their decisions, but in this case I felt particularly frustrated that we could do nothing more than we were doing.

The last time I saw Milagros was the week before Christmas 1986, when she came to what was to be her last prenatal visit. After missing another three or four appointments, she had finally returned to be seen once more. She had not gained any weight since her previous visit and was feeling very weak. When I told her I wanted to hospitalize her, she looked at me with tired eyes and told me she would think about it. She touched my arm as she left, smiled almost imperceptibly, and thanked me for trying to help her— a gesture that was very much out of character for her.

A couple of days later I was watching the 11 o'clock news, with its litany of murders, fires, and other local disasters, and I heard, disbelieving at first, that one of the night's stories concerned Milagros. As I later found out, Milagros had gotten into an argument with a customer in the doorway of a tenement in Mott Haven, a neighborhood at the southern tip of the South Bronx. The argument ended with Milagros getting her throat slit and collapsing in a pool of blood on the ground. Someone called 911, and she was brought to Lincoln Hospital, where she was dead on arrival in the emergency room. The EMTs had continued cardiopulmonary resuscitation, even though it was futile, in the hope that the baby—then thirty-six weeks—might still be saved. A postmortem emergency cesarean section was performed in the ER, and the baby was still alive, but barely. It died after twenty-four hours in the neonatal intensive care unit.

This was not the first time, or the last, that I ever felt helpless, angry, or guilty over my inability to save a patient from his or her demons, but I still remember vividly my few encounters with Milagros and her unborn baby. It was as if the mother was already halfway home, on her way back to another world, while the baby wanted to stay, to be born, yet couldn't. Their paths were meant to diverge, but they remained harnessed together, literally, by the uncut umbilical cord. In order to survive, babies normally need to be merged with their mothers in utero; in this case, it was as if the baby needed to be separated from its mother so as not to die with her. Like spectators peering into the shadows, we could make out the outline of this new creature, nameless, faceless, filled with life yet surrounded by death, but we could not free it.

Before Milagros, I had never known life and death to coexist so intimately, so interdependently. This was something that later reverberated deeply with my own history, as I became aware of the meaning of my father's death in my own life. In an inversion of the image of Milagros and her baby, in which life was surrounded by death, for me there was something dead inside, hidden away, that I needed to bring out into the light if I was to survive.

Another patient still vivid in my memory is Delia, a beautiful young Puerto Rican woman—fresh-faced, a little waiflike, with intense brown eyes that sparkled when she smiled. I saw her for the first time when she was approximately ten weeks pregnant, after she had started to have some abdominal cramping and intermittent vaginal bleeding. The pregnancy was her first, and she was worried that she would lose the baby—especially, as she told me tearfully, because the father, her boyfriend of five years, had been shot and killed four weeks before. I sent her home on bed rest and checked in with her by phone over the next several days. (Fortunately, unlike many of our patients, Delia had a stable apartment and was able to afford and maintain a telephone.) Gradually, over the course of a long, tense week, the cramps subsided and the bleeding stopped. She began to gain weight, and at her eighteen-week visit we were able to hear the baby's heartbeat with the ultrasonic fetal stethoscope.

Delia had tested HIV positive a couple of months before becoming pregnant, and it had never occurred to her not to keep the pregnancy. After the bleeding episode, she did well during the remainder of her pregnancy and was proud of the progress that she was making. Delia became very close with Carmen, who was pregnant at around the same time, and Magaly, who played the role of wise older sister to the other two, having already been through this several times. I still remember the three of them walking into my office in the clinic one day, arm in arm, laughing as they kept interrupting each other in their excitement to tell me about an idea they had to start a support group for pregnant women with HIV. It felt as if I was a high school teacher and they were three of my favorite students who had come in to tell me about their plans for the senior prom—I was touched by the way they seemed, for a moment, so unburdened of the gripping heaviness of their daily lives, so easy in their sisterly care for each other.

After a pregnancy that was uneventful after the early bleeding episode, Delia delivered a healthy, normal-weight baby boy at full term. She named him Michael after his father, whose name had been Miguel. Delia then passed many anxious months, waiting to see whether or not the baby was infected, waiting to see whether Michael's positive HIV antibody test would turn negative. This waiting period was made even more poignant by the fact, which I discovered only after Delia gave birth, that her own mother, herself an intravenous drug user in her late forties, was sick and dying from AIDS. Michael continued to grow and develop normally, gaining weight, and went through the normal developmental milestones of infancy. In contrast, Delia's own health began to decline during the child's first year. She became progressively weaker, lost her energy and some of her alertness, and had to be hospitalized for a bacterial pneumonia. We seemed to be watching a transformation or transfer of energy,

as the mother became more and more depleted of life while the infant became filled with it.

By the time the baby was eighteen months old, we were fairly certain
that he was free of infection from the virus: his HIV antibody test had become negative and remained so after nine months of age, all his other
blood tests had remained normal, and his growth and development continued to be in normal range. But at the same time, Delia herself was fad-
ing; she seemed unlikely to survive the child's second birthday. I remember sitting at a case conference with our clinic medical and social work
staff, considering the options for care of the baby after Delia's death. None
of them seemed very good, and we did not have a clear plan in place. As I
sat at the meeting, I had a strong urge, which I felt intensely but did not
understand rationally, to declare that I myself would care for this parent-
less child as a foster parent. As I thought about it, this idea seemed utterly
crazy and inappropriate, but that did not diminish the urge. Fortunately, I
did not act on it at the time. I mentioned it that night to Nancy, who was
able to put it in an appropriate perspective: "What, are you nuts?" And indeed I could not even imagine how this would be remotely possible. Our
own daughters were one and three years old at the time, both of us were
working full-time, I was more often than not working late, traveling, or
otherwise unavailable, and there were a thousand other reasons that this
would never work. Yet I became aware of my deep desire to be a father to
this lost boy.

Fortunately, within a couple of weeks, Delia came in and told me that
her own father, who lived in San Juan and with whom she had had only in-
frequent contact in recent years, had said that he and his new wife would
take care of Delia and, eventually, her baby. This was a wonderful, unexpected solution, and I was happy and relieved that her father had suddenly
reappeared to resolve the crisis. But I also noticed a twinge of regret and
disappointment—as inappropriate as it was—that I would not be playing
this role myself. Unconsciously, my yearning to parent this child was a dis-

placement of my yearning for the father that had never been present in my life. Without realizing it, Delia helped me to identify that aching need.

When I first met Javon, I felt as though I was in the presence of royalty. He was homeless, living on the subway, wearing tattered clothing, but he seemed like an African prince who absentmindedly had wandered away from his kingdom. He was six-foot-four and well-muscled, with chestnut-colored skin and a striking, high-cheekboned profile. (His grandmother, he once told me, had been a full-blooded Cherokee.) Javon was HIV infected, but his immediate problem, which also accounted for his marginal living situation, was that he had become addicted to crack and had lost his job, his home, and his family in pursuit of the drug. Although he had been an IV drug user for years in the past, he had been clean for five years until crack hit the streets. He quickly became addicted and, like many of our patients, ended up becoming readdicted to heroin as well, using it to modulate some of the more unpleasant symptoms—jitteriness, insomnia, racing thoughts, feeling "wired"—frequently caused by heavy crack use.

Unlike many patients whose lives had been turned upside down by crack but who vehemently denied that they were even using the drug, Javon was always completely open and honest about his addiction. It was as if the layers of denial, deception, and guile that served to cover up the true feelings of many of our patients had in him been neatly stripped away to reveal a disarmingly healthy personality structure. He would come in and talk about his crack binges and his inability to control them with the same clinical, dispassionate perspective that William Burroughs captured so well in *Naked Lunch*, when he describes the old-timer Tangier opium addict inspecting his scarred, wooden skin for a place to inject with the impartial, expert eye of a horse trader sizing up a new prospect. But in spite of Javon's honesty and willingness to seek help for his cocaine addiction, there was no effective treatment available.

A new level of desperation had set in within the South Bronx communities around our clinics following the advent of crack in 1986. Within just a few months, we became acutely aware—both treatment program staff and patients—of this new drug, which was unlike anything we had seen before. This wasn't simply a case of high-purity heroin or synthetic Fentanyl resulting in more overdoses on the street than expected. This was something new, powerful, and uncontrollable. I began to hear horror stories from some of the old "dope fiends"—a term that some of our older patients used to describe themselves, with not a little pride—recounting how crack "takes your heart" in a way that they had never experienced. Old addicts who had withdrawn cold turkey from heroin countless times in basement apartments, in jail, or on the street, testified that you could not walk away from this new drug and described in vivid detail how it just kept coming after you.

Unlike heroin, for which even heavy users tended to modulate their use, generally not exceeding four doses per day, users of cocaine (and especially crack) were more likely to engage in binges—going "on a mission" was the common phrase—using up to twenty times a day or more for days at a time before the inevitable crash. Any heroin addict could tell you in an instant how many times a day he used the drug. Asking the same question of a cocaine addict often produced a puzzled stare as he slowly counted up all the fingers on both hands and then lost track. Although the chemistry of the drug is the same, crack cocaine is in a different universe from intranasal, powdered cocaine, which was synonymous with the fast-paced glamour world of Manhattan and the conspicuous consumption of the boom years of the 1980s. Far from Studio 54, glittering midtown hotels, and Wall Street executive suites, crack defined a world of vermin-infested crack houses, boarded-up tenements, and glass-strewn lots, a sordid world in which parents would sell or abandon their children for their next pipeful, in which crack and AIDS had teamed up to produce a new legion of walking dead.

The grim efficiency with which the AIDS virus had circulated through the drug-using community was now matched by the physiologic effectiveness of smoked cocaine: the lung-to-brain transit time for the smoked drug was much quicker than that from the peripheral veins of the forearm to the brain when the drug was injected. This was an important feature, for the intensity of a drug's effect—the "rush"—is often dependent on how quickly it gets into the brain. The new crack product was also reported to be much safer to use than smoking "freebase" cocaine, whose most celebrated victim at the time was Richard Pryor.

Indeed, the arrival of crack on the streets of the Bronx was truly a triumph in marketing. Here was a drug that was relatively cheap (five dollars a vial), easy to use, and immediately effective, a combination that created a cadre of loyal, compulsive users who would do anything to keep getting more. As a testament to the power and pervasiveness of this new product, the sidewalks and gutters of the streets around our clinics were soon littered with the empty little plastic vials and their brightly colored stoppers, like a beach strewn with the debris of a turbulent sea.

Some observers hoped, cynically, that the advent of crack would result in a decrease in needle use and thus a decreased risk of HIV transmission among drug users. Unfortunately, the opposite turned out to be true, due to two factors. The first was increased risk of sexual transmission associated with crack use. Because crack inspires a more frantic urgency than heroin and is more likely to be consumed in binges, young women became particularly vulnerable to sexual exploitation. (A girl of no more than seventeen once stumbled up to my car outside a crack house near our clinic and told me I could do whatever I wanted with her for a dollar.) The second was the fact that, as in Javon's case, uncontrolled crack use often led to an increased use of injected heroin as a means of trying to calm down from the speedlike feelings produced by the cocaine.

The only way that Javon could ever manage to stop smoking crack for any length of time was by getting arrested for turnstile jumping or some other minor offense and going to Rikers Island. (New York City's major detention center, Rikers Island processes more than 120,000 admissions per year.) Ironically, Javon once told me that he was considering getting arrested again, after he had already stopped using crack for a while, because he did not have an active Medicaid card. He couldn't afford his AZT, and he knew he would get it if he were incarcerated and under the care of the Rikers Island Health Service. (The Rikers Island Health Service was also operated by Montefiore Hospital, and several of my good friends ran the program. We periodically conferred about "frequent fliers," patients who shuttled back and forth between the methadone program and the detention center. We would arrange follow-up tests and avoid duplication of diagnostic workups in much the same way that physicians in nursing homes and hospitals confer on the efficient comanagement of their elderly patients.)

What finally helped break the cycle for Javon was that he was lucky enough to be accepted as a resident in Bailey House, a renovated rooming house on Christopher Street in Greenwich Village, right off the West Side Highway next to the Hudson River. This had recently been refurbished and established as a residence for people with AIDS, supported by an enormous outpouring of love and support from the local gay community. Many of the rooms had beautiful interior designs and furnishings, and local florists kept a bountiful supply of fresh flowers in bloom throughout the facility. The building had a rooftop terrace, where the residents sometimes had barbecues in summer and where they could sit in the evening and watch the boats on the river and the twinkling lights across the Hudson on the New Jersey shore. Javon used to joke with me that he felt that he had already died and gone to heaven: for the first time in his recent memory, he had a room of his own, his own telephone line, the promise of three meals a day, and warmth from the cold without being in a prison or homeless shelter.

By a tremendous act of will, and also through simple good manners—he told me that he thought it would show disrespect to his beautiful new surroundings if he were to continue to be strung out on crack—Javon stopped all his drug use and began going to daily Narcotics Anonymous meetings. At the same time he began to get sick. First he developed tuberculosis—which he had probably contracted while on the street or in jail—and then he was hospitalized for nearly a month for a severe deep tissue infection involving muscle and surrounding tissue in his thighs. Through all this, he maintained his sobriety, and he seemed with each new challenge to be even more proud of having overcome his addiction. Several months later, after he was out of the hospital and back at Bailey House but becoming progressively weaker from AIDS-related wasting, he told me how gratified he was to have relearned what it was like to live in the world as a responsible adult; he was only sorry that he had to die in order to make the discovery.

Once he cleaned up, Javon got back in touch with his sixteen-year-old son, who had been living with an aunt in Philadelphia. Monroe was his only son, and, when I met him in the hospital during one of his father's illnesses, I was struck immediately both by their strong resemblance to each other and by the powerful bond between them. About six months before he died, Javon asked me solemnly how much longer I thought he had to live, because there were many things he still needed to teach his son before he died. I told him, as I always do, that no one can predict, but that I thought it could be between six months and a year. He breathed a heavy sigh of relief and told me that this was a big load off his mind because he was afraid that anything less might not be sufficient.

Javon was friendly with several other patients in the clinic who had all been diagnosed with AIDS at around the same time. I remember sitting next to him at the funeral of one of his friends, also my patient, in a small funeral home in a West Indian neighborhood on White Plains Road near Gun Hill. As I followed him up to the casket to view Carol's body, I felt a shudder, realizing how courageous it was for him just to be there, knowing that *he* knew that he would soon be in the same place.

Javon never told me, and I never asked him, whether he had passed on everything that he had intended to tell his son. I assume that he did, because when he finally died he seemed to be at peace. What had struck me was his conscious commitment to leave a legacy for his son, to help initiate him into manhood, and to let him know how much he cared about him. This commitment of a father to his son, to help him grow up and go out into the world as a man, was something I had never had. These were precious gifts, and I found myself feeling very alone, wanting to hold onto these gifts for myself as I listened to Javon speak about his son. Although I didn't share this with Javon at the time—looking back, I probably should have—I also felt a little sad and jealous of his son for having such a concerned and loving father.

One of my favorite patients was Betty, a thirty-three-year-old Puerto Rican woman whom I first met because she was causing such behavior problems at the methadone clinic that her counselor was ready to terminate her from the program. She was loud, demanding, articulate, and extremely manipulative, and she was an expert at making everyone run around at cross purposes while she sat calmly in the eye of the storm—an "egg beater," as we called such patients. It was apparent from the moment I met her that Betty was also smart, funny, suspicious, and, most of all, terrified about her illness and what she feared it would do to her. Betty's ten-year-old daughter, whom she had entrusted to her mother's care, was starting to show some early signs of preadolescent troublemaking in school.

Betty had also had some recent problems with cocaine use. She was afraid that she might be kicked off the methadone program and have to go back to supporting her heroin addiction by working the streets near Hunt's Point Terminal Market in the southeast Bronx. After meeting together with her counselor and the program administrator, we made a deal: we would write up a contract specifying what behaviors would and would not be tolerated, as well as the obligation of the program to retain her in treatment as long as she complied with her part of the agreement. It was decided that I would continue to be her doctor—that I would, in fact, be the only medical person she would interact with, to avoid further miscommunication.

This arrangement worked remarkably well over the next several months. Betty's behavior improved, the frequency of her cocaine-positive urines decreased, and there were fewer complaints about her from clinic staff. One day, however, she became sick. This was in the years before prophylaxis against *Pneumocystis carinii* pneumonia had become standard, and PCP was still the most common illness and cause of death among AIDS patients. (Now it's almost completely preventable.) Betty had noticed a mild cough for a couple of weeks, along with some slowly progressive shortness of breath. Finally, she was unable even to walk upstairs to get to her apartment or to perform even minimal housework without having to sit down to rest. She was admitted to the hospital with what looked like a classic case of PCP, and after a few days began to respond to the IV therapy. At that point, however, she became more and more angry and abusive with nursing staff, accusing them of withholding her methadone or diluting it, and finding fault with even the most trivial details of the hospital routine. The floor nursing staff, who had not known Betty before she had become ill, quickly assessed her as another ungrateful, foul-mouthed drug addict. In the passive-aggressive ways that hospital staff members sometimes react when they don't like a patient, they began to put up their own barriers against her.

Finally, even these defenses were no longer working, and the head nurse asked me to come up to the floor to speak to Betty. ("*Your* patient," she emphasized, as if to distance herself even further from Betty's distasteful behavior.) When I got off the elevator, I was met by a trio of floor nurses, all experienced caregivers, who smiled as they greeted me but could not fully conceal their disgusted conviction that it was somehow my fault that such a patient should exist to make their lives so miserable.

This was a response that I had gotten used to in the hospital. Over the years I had become identified as that doctor in the methadone program who took care of all "those" drug addicts. Being the physician for this large group of drug users meant being tainted by some of the same negative associations that were directed toward the patients themselves. Although my interactions with nurses and my physician colleagues at the hospital were, in general, excellent, at times I felt that some of them would prefer never to have to deal with me or my difficult and demanding patients again. A friend of mine once told me of a Department of Medicine administrative meeting in the hospital, at which someone brought up a problem that had occurred in the ER the night before. A drunken and disheveled homeless patient had shown up and started acting abusively toward the nursing staff. Someone else at the meeting then joked, to everyone's amusement, "Oh, it must have been one of Peter *Selwyn's* patients!"

There was an unspoken double standard in the hospital, which often made it very frustrating trying to schedule certain tests or have procedures performed for patients from the methadone program. On a rare occasion, someone would come right out and declare a hatred for drug addicts or an opinion that they didn't deserve the best care: the chief of one of the noninvasive diagnostic testing services once told me, in perverse ignorance of basic infection control, that he didn't want his equipment contaminated by our patients; and a few surgeons refused outright to operate on our patients with AIDS. More often, though, these prejudices were expressed subtly— we were made to feel as though we were begging for crumbs, always having to go to the end of the line.

Of course, it didn't help when our patients refused to cooperate with a procedure or failed to show up for an appointment that we had pleaded for. These transgressions only served to confirm the hospital staff's prejudices and left us feeling foolish, caught in the middle. Sometimes it was even worse, like the time I cajoled the staff at the Family Health Center, my former training site, to let me bring over some of my pregnant patients from the methadone program to have sonograms done there. This was before the Family Health Center itself became a major site for providing HIV care in the local community, and the staff members there were still wary because they hadn't yet seen many drug-addicted patients with AIDS. They finally agreed, but one of the first patients I sent over—Marta, in fact, whom I introduced above—promptly stole a staff member's pocketbook that had been left in a drawer in the examining room.

On the day that the head nurse had asked me to come speak with Betty, I went to the end of the hall to the single isolation room where she was being kept due to her boisterous behavior. When I opened the door, I found that the drawers of her nightstand had been emptied on the floor and her bedclothes flung wildly about the room. Betty stood by the side of her bed, holding her IV pole like Neptune holding his trident, as if she were daring me to come into the room.

I walked in and asked her permission to sit on the edge of the bed. She launched into a five-minute tirade about the injustices she had suffered at the hands of the floor nurses. ("I never get my methadone on time, plus they're cutting it with something. Whenever I call they never come, and this food tastes like they're trying to poison me, and no one tells me a goddamn thing about what is going on. . . .") My first impulse was to stop her and point out that each accusation she was making was either untrue or explainable by the inscrutable logic of hospital routine. But something made me hold back. I simply sat and listened to what she had to say. After she was finished, she looked at me quizzically, expecting me to respond. I simply looked back at her and nodded, waiting for her to go on.

Betty took a Kleenex box and threw it across the room, exclaiming that she was tired of being treated like a dirty junkie. I nodded again, and she responded by sliding her breakfast tray over onto the floor, with a clash of silverware, her orange juice spilling into a slowly widening circle on the linoleum tiles. I continued to sit, wordless, simply being present.

Finally, when she had run out of things to complain about, I said quietly, "I think I would be pretty upset, too, if I had just been diagnosed with PCP and was worried about how long I was going to live." Betty looked at me, and then immediately started to cry, continuing for ten minutes, inconsolably, going through half of the Kleenex box, which I had placed back on her bed next to her. When she was finished crying, she looked up at me and began to talk about her real fears of dying, of losing her daughter, of being rejected by her mother's family. We talked for another half hour while I acknowledged her fears and told her that we would work with her to address them. We also talked about how she would do a lot better and be more likely to get what she wanted if she behaved herself on the unit. On my way out, I told the head nurse that I thought things would start to get better.

Within two days, the same nurses who had been looking for excuses to get Betty to sign herself out of the hospital against medical advice were now going to the coffee shop to get doughnuts for her on their lunch breaks. It was a miraculous transformation, and it taught me, more than any other experience, the importance of simply being there for patients, as a sympathetic companion, not as a judge, commentator, or rescuer. I could have stopped Betty's diatribe and bluntly informed her that her behavior was unacceptable, probably provoking her to act out even more and leave the hospital. Or I could have simply withdrawn myself and told her that I could not help her as long as she acted in this way. None of these responses would have resulted in a meaningful solution to the problem of Betty's behavior, and her unresolved fears and conflicts would have erupted in some other manner, probably in a short period of time. I was reminded of the wisdom of one of my first teachers in medical school, a silver-haired emeritus professor of medicine at Harvard, who gave the sage advice that I have always tried to remember at times like this: "Don't just do something, sit there!"

Betty went on to recover fully from PCP and became very involved in her follow-up medical care. She traveled around the Bronx with a waist pack full of her medication bottles, a schedule for each dose, and a programmable alarm clock that went off to alert her when it was time for her next pill. Before she had been discharged from the hospital, she had told her mother that she had AIDS; her mother embraced her lovingly and pledged to continue to take care of her and her daughter. Betty also regained her wry, mordant sense of humor. When a young emergency room intern asked her during a routine exam whether she had any health problems, she replied, "No, honey, aside from having AIDS, I am really very healthy." One day she asked me conspiratorially, "Dr. Selwyn, how come white guys always look like they have a bag of shit in the back of their pants?" And she played an increasingly active role in our clinic support groups and the growing buddy system of women helping their peers.

Betty and I had an easy, joking relationship, and we genuinely liked each other. I remember one time when a stethoscope disappeared in the clinic and the rumor was that a patient had taken it. Betty told me that she didn't know anything about it. I believed her, but she kept insisting, "But Dr. Selwyn, I don't want you to think that I'm a thief!" I laughed and replied, "But Betty, I *know* you're a thief, and I still love you!" and gave her a hug.

Betty's last illness came quickly, and she became rapidly demented and unable to walk over a period of weeks. The rapidity of this course suggested to us that she had one of the more devastating brain infections of

AIDS, progressive multifocal leukoencephalopathy (PML), instead of the more common, indolent dementia associated with AIDS itself. There was no treatment for PML—even now, treatment is marginally effective at best—and, mercifully, patients usually did not survive very long after they had become afflicted. The last time I saw Betty alive, she was propped up in her hospital bed, a teddy bear at her side, her arms and legs twitching in little involuntary jerks. I went into her room, sat by her bed, and began, on a sudden impulse, to feed her with a spoon from her tray.

I felt suddenly as if this was the most important thing I could do for her at that moment, though I had a distinctly uncomfortable feeling that it would be embarrassing for me if a group of my colleagues were suddenly to come by and see me feeding her. (How odd, that such a simple act of nurturing should seem so out of place for a physician.) I fed Betty some Cream of Wheat, which she slurped up eagerly, reminding me of one of my daughters. I wiped the small dribble of Cream of Wheat from her lower lip with the spoon in the same way that I had done so many times at home. Then I held her hand, sat with her, said goodbye, and left. Once again, I realized with Betty that one of the most important services I could offer as a physician had more to do with being there than with anything else.

At her funeral, Betty was laid out in a delicate white lace dress. She looked like an angel as I looked down at her in the open casket. Her daughter sat on a chair in the front row, next to her grandmother, her hair tied up in a tight knot in the back, swinging her legs back and forth slowly, her toes almost touching the floor. I looked at her and hoped that she would have the same yearning and zest for life that her mother had had. Betty truly helped me to understand what it means to embrace life, and to see that the work that we do and the impact that we have in the world are measured only, finally, in the people whose lives we touch.

❋

Even as I finish recalling the lives and deaths of these five patients—Nelson, Milagros, Delia, Javon, and Betty—I am reminded of many others, people whose stories or struggles or special qualities struck me in some lasting way. But these five were the ones who affected me the most and helped me to unlock a secret in my own life that I had been only dimly aware of before. During the time that I was working with these patients as their care provider, I made no conscious connection for the most part between aspects of their lives and my own: but each touched something in my heart that, like repeated efforts to kindle a fire, finally took hold.

Each of them, in his or her own way, led me to realize the importance of my own history and feelings concerning my father, his death, and my life. They helped me to start the journey back to reclaim that history, to understand it, to experience it, and finally to put it in perspective. Before I met these five patients, I lived my life with a void inside that I did not even know was there: they helped me both to recognize that void and to begin the long process of filling it in. For this, I will always be grateful to them, and, like most situations in which I felt I have been truly helpful and giving to patients, I have felt simultaneously that I received much more from them in return.

I also feel that I owe a special debt to all my drug-using patients for helping me understand the nature of addiction and the ways that addiction is often a shield that covers unresolved pain. Not until I had spent several years around heroin addicts was I able to realize that certain aspects of my work life were very similar to their patterns of addictive behavior: one's whole life organized around the activity (shooting up or working) to the exclusion of other people and activities; the intense gratification during the activity and the profound letdown once it is over (binging on the drug or writing a grant proposal); the craving of something outside oneself to feel whole and satisfied (obtaining heroin to avoid withdrawal, getting a paper published in the *New England Journal of Medicine*); and the constant anxiety of being on the edge, just short of being overwhelmed by the constant demands of this all-defining activity, which has taken on a life of its own.

Working with drug addicts brings out some of health care providers' worst fears, prejudices, and feelings of powerlessness. More fundamentally, it gives us the opportunity to confront some of the least attractive and most dysfunctional aspects of our own behaviors, with the possibility of recognizing and seeking to change them. It also forces us to witness in others certain primitive behaviors that we have been duly taught to suppress over many years of socialization and training—pleasure seeking, instant gratification, selfishness, irresponsibility, an inability to tolerate pain or anxiety—which may also account for the often visceral aversion that health care providers feel toward drug addicts.

It is arrogant for a doctor to presume—yet we do it all the time—that we can suddenly put a stop to a patient's drug addiction, which by the time we first see the patient has become a powerful, biologically reinforced behavior that has lasted for years if not decades. Yet how often have I heard well-meaning health professionals in a hospital or emergency room solemnly advise a drug injector to stop shooting up because it's bad for his health—thinking that this had perhaps not yet occurred to him—and then reacting with dismay and disgust when the patient returns to the hospital a month later with a new complication of drug injection.

If, instead, we come to understand addiction as a chronic, conditioned set of behaviors, which persist despite the knowledge of adverse consequences, reinforced by denial, shame, fear, and often physical dependence, we realize that this is not something that will go away by itself. We realize also that doctors do not have the power to exorcise this demon, nor is it a sign of our personal failure if we are unable miraculously to do so. This phenomenon is beyond blame and morality: whether it is defined as an illness, a condition, or a behavior, drug addiction is not something in which the patient has become engaged specifically in order to make things difficult for us. And lastly, importantly, we realize that none of our patients can begin the long and difficult process of recovery from addiction until they are ready to do so themselves. Our role as care providers is to be there, to bear witness, to be willing to accompany patients through their illness, and to refrain from passing judgment. Neither can we save them nor do we have the right to condemn them.

The surrender of our omnipotence—the illusion of being able to control the outcome, the feeling of having to win, in some sense—is an important first step in becoming effective care providers. These feelings and needs always stand in the way of true empathy and caring. It is often counterintuitive, but one day it suddenly dawns on you that you can set limits without being punitive, that you can be an effective caregiver for the patient without having to control the outcome, and that at a certain point you must offer your support and advice and then simply let it go without judgment or blame.

More than fifteen years later, I still find it very challenging and gratifying to work with HIV-infected drug users. Notwithstanding all the issues that I have discussed, there *is* something special about the satisfaction for the care provider when patients perceive, perhaps indeed for the first time in their lives, that someone in a white coat is treating them with concern and respect. There is also something breathtaking about the process of recovery from addiction. Admittedly, it does not happen frequently, but when it does, it is a privilege to witness patients overcome demons that have pursued them for years. Given the conditions of poverty, marginalization, and social deterioration in which many of our patients are obliged to live, I continue to be humbled and amazed by the courage and determination of those who are able to overcome these barriers and their addiction. At moments like this, I cannot imagine any other work that would be as fulfilling.

# 3 Excavation

Not until late 1987, after I had been caring for AIDS patients for more than six years, did it finally dawn on me what personal meaning the AIDS epidemic held for me. Surrounded by so much suffering and death, especially with the tenuous boundaries I have described between myself and my patients, I became enmeshed in certain ways with their lives: overinvolvement with work, nightmares and loss of sleep, and feelings of either omnipotence or total vulnerability when patients either survived an episode of illness or died despite all efforts. In other respects, emotionally, I remained somewhat detached. Sometimes detachment is healthy and appropriate for a physician, as long as one does not hide behind it; it is important to maintain appropriate boundaries, for the well-being of both parties. Sometimes, though, detachment—a certain closing off of the heart—can be a sign of one's own unresolved emotional pain, which has been buried under layers of denial, socialization, and professional competence.

One day, close to Christmas 1987, I attended a concert at the Cathedral of St. John the Divine in Manhattan, near Columbia University. As I was leaving the church, I noticed a place along one of the side walls of the church where many candles were burning on a small table, in front of a plain white scroll. On the scroll, in calligraphy, were the simple words, "In memory of those who have died of AIDS." I stopped and stared at those words, and suddenly everything seemed real in a way that it had never seemed before. At that moment, I felt something opening that had been closed off in me, and I suddenly began to cry for all the patients I had lost, whose faces I could see through the flickering light of the candles. I realized then that this work was about me and my life in ways that I had not understood.

Elisabeth Kübler-Ross, who has been one of my most important teachers, once said, "You never cry for anyone else, you only cry for yourself." After my experience in the cathedral, I came to understand the meaning of this simple phrase.

My father died suddenly at the age of thirty-five, when I was eighteen months old, on October 17, 1955. He was an accountant, and he fell to his death from the window of an office building in lower Manhattan; for my entire childhood, this was as much as I knew about him, his life, and his death. Because of the unusual circumstances of his death, this event and even the memory of his life quickly became family secrets that I was not permitted to discuss, so in effect, I experienced a double loss. In some ways, I had come to believe that maybe he had never even existed. It is perhaps a testimony of the many layers of denial and avoidance with which my family—and I myself—had covered up his death, that it wasn't until six years into the AIDS epidemic that I ever connected my work with any conscious thoughts about my father.

As I gradually reconstructed the story, piece by piece, with many gaping holes remaining, my father most likely died by suicide and not, as I had grown up believing, in a bizarre accident in which he inexplicably lost his balance and fell out of a window. The starker truth, which was also ultimately more believable than what I had been told as a child, was that he did not fall, but jumped.

It was not until more than thirty years later—when I was confronted with the deaths of all these young men and women whom I could no more save than I could have saved my father—that I began to realize that I had never come to terms with this first and primal loss. After my revelation in the cathedral, I suddenly understood why I was so attracted to lost causes, why I had been drawn so repeatedly to the bedsides of my dying patients, why I always felt, no matter how hard I tried, that I was not doing enough. I suddenly understood why I felt that I had failed whenever a patient died, as if this was something that I should have been able to prevent, when in fact, I could not.

This process of coming to terms with my past was not easy, but I am convinced that it saved my life, or that at the very least it enabled me to give up a burden that I had carried for almost thirty-five years without even having been aware of its presence. Once I had made that simple and profound connection, I was amazed that it had not occurred to me sooner.

How many times had I sat at the bedside of dying young fathers, feeling their pain and that of their soon-to-be orphaned children, without making the simple association between their life histories and my own. How fitting that I should have chosen family medicine as my specialty, after growing up not only in a family that had been broken by the violent death of the father, but one in which the very notion of family history seemed to be a source of pain or discomfort.

My mother worked tirelessly to make life safe and comfortable for me, and I am convinced that to this day she would, without a second's hesitation, jump in front of a speeding truck to save me, her only son. My mother's parents, especially my grandfather, were also very much a part of our family unit. All memories of my father, however, seemed tainted and suspect. Even the mention of his name caused nervous fidgeting and downcast eyes. By extension, my father's family—his parents, his two sisters and their families—must all have been too vivid a reminder of his death for my mother to feel comfortable with them. Only recently, after decades of no contact, have I begun to reestablish a connection with relatives on my father's side. His family, like my mother, seemed only too willing to suppress his memory and were equally uncomfortable discussing his death. (I now know that for some of them it remains a fresh wound, even after years of denial, as raw and searing as the day it happened, more than forty years ago.)

In this environment I learned that it wasn't acceptable to ask about certain things, and that family secrets are better left undisturbed, lest they cause further pain. Not surprising, then, that I should have found the lives of my patients in the AIDS epidemic so compelling: the idealized family trinity of Nelson, his wife, and son; Milagros's spiral of self-destruction, which we were helpless to prevent, and from which her baby could not escape; the vulnerability of Delia's infant child, on the verge of being abandoned, an orphan in need of a parent; Javon's earnest desire to leave a conscious legacy for his son; Betty's intense yearning for life—she would never have contemplated suicide—even and especially while staring in the face of death.

How fitting, also, was my more fundamental choice to work in the AIDS epidemic, to which I had gravitated without consciously knowing why.

Here I was in my early thirties, a new father, my own father having died at age thirty-five when I was an infant, and now I was surrounded by dying thirty-five-year olds, widows, orphaned children. The thought did not occur to me consciously, but I am certain that on some level, with the magical thinking of the two-year-old whose daddy has gone away, I believed that maybe he would come back if I was able to save my patients. If I was good enough, or expert enough—if I was omnipotent—I could either *make* him come home or he would want to come back himself.

I began to see further connections: AIDS, the most compelling contemporary example of a stigmatizing illness, is linked to behaviors that themselves are stigmatized and kept hidden by society. Suicide, which is still a powerful symbol of stigma for the survivors, is something that doesn't happen in "good" families, something that must be kept secret so that those who remain aren't further tainted by the suspicion that somehow the moral failings represented by the disease also extend to them. Secrecy deepens the hidden wound for the survivors: on the outside everything looks normal, and they must suppress any sign of what has happened, which only furthers their isolation. Maintaining this facade of normalcy demands psychic energy and takes its toll from those who are left behind: it becomes *their* problem, *their* fault, *their* secret. I envied my patients' reconciliations with their families, the opportunities that they had come to terms, to say what had to be said, to hold each other one last time, to say goodbye. In these ways, they were often able to overcome some of the stigma of their disease, to achieve some measure of closure.

For people who commit suicide and their families, there are no such reconciliations, there is no such leave taking or closure. Suicide is not usually intended to hurt anyone else; yet unlike AIDS, suicide is almost always experienced by the survivors as an assault, a betrayal, a deliberate abandonment. For AIDS and suicide alike, though, both those who die and those who survive are too often clouded by shame, opprobrium, and the fearful impulse to remain silent. How appropriate then, for me to be drawn so strongly to the side of my dying, drug-addicted AIDS patients, from whom the outside world recoiled in such disgust and horror. How necessary, then, for me to tell my own story, to let out the secret that was hidden behind the facade.

In some respects, I did not fully appreciate the impact of my father's death until I became a father myself and realized, by seeing the central role that I played in my children's lives and development, how gaping this absence must have been in my own. I remember my mother once telling me that, for several months after my father died, I would stand by the window and call for him, using whatever limited speech I had at the time, until one day I finally stopped. I pictured that little boy, through the lens of my own relationship with my children, and felt his loss all the more deeply.

Seeing my children grow up, strong, bright, and healthy, I also became aware that each of the milestones I celebrated with them had gone unnoticed by my father in my own life. I suddenly felt that, after learning to walk and saying a few words, everything I had accomplished had been on my own. Of course, that was not completely true—my mother and grandparents had been there—but as I felt my growing presence in my own children's lives, I also felt, poignantly, my father's profound absence from my own. Learning how to read, to throw a ball, to ride a bicycle, to play tennis: these were all things that I suddenly yearned to be able to show him, to share with him, along with the underlying, intense need to have him be proud of me and my successful journey through life thus far.

At the same time, I became aware of a great void where all the things that a father should teach a boy should be. I felt this absence especially when talking to a patient like Javon about his hopes for his son and the things that he needed to teach him, or hearing another patient describe, in careful detail, his plans for creating a videotape library to pass on to his children, each volume timed to be viewed at a different developmental stage in their lives.

That day in the Cathedral of St. John the Divine, I felt as if I had suddenly opened up a hidden well inside of me, a source of feelings, thoughts, and memories that had been covered over for decades, a wellspring I had not even known was there. Over the following weeks, months, and even years, I would explore these long-forgotten emotions. Once the well had been opened, it couldn't be sealed over again, even if I had wanted it to be.

As part of coming to terms with my father's death, I felt that I had to understand his life, so I tried to make an inventory of everything I knew about him. I had been told that he had a good sense of humor, that he was articulate, that he had bad eyesight and needed to wear thick glasses, that he had childhood mastoid infections that affected his hearing. He was a good tennis player. He loved English literature but became an accountant instead of a teacher because he needed to support his family. He was a middle sibling, with an older and younger sister, and was the darling of the family when growing up. His parents had come to the United States as children from Russia, part of the wave of eastern European Jews who immigrated here at the end of the nineteenth century. His father Harry worked in a factory in New York's garment district.

My father was born Aaron Srebnik in New York City on January 15, 1920, and changed his last name to Selwyn when he was twenty-five. I always wondered whether this bespoke a lack of self-acceptance on his part, or a feeling of not belonging. I still do not know how he came up with the name Selwyn, by which, with one stroke of the pen, he symbolically seemed to have stepped from the shadow of the shtetl to the ranks of the English aristocracy. I once came across the poem "To Hugh Selwyn Mauberley," by Ezra Pound, and scrutinized it line by line, fantasizing that this might give me the answer, but it didn't.

My father went to Haaren High School on Manhattan's West Side, and,

like my grandfather, went to City College, graduating in 1941. He met my
mother a few years later, before the end of World War II—he had been
rejected for military service because of his eyesight and poor hearing.
They were married at the Essex House Hotel on Central Park South in
1946. I have a photograph of all four of my grandparents with my parents—that sounds like such an odd phrase to me; I almost never use the
term "my parents"—on their wedding day, standing in front of the stone
wall facade on 59th Street, Central Park South. I once walked the length
of that wall to try to find the exact location where the picture was taken,
hoping somehow that I could share in this convergence of heredity, this
coming together of my most immediate ancestors.

In addition to these scattered bits of information about my father, I also
had been told by both my mother and my aunts that he loved me very
much, and that he felt I was his greatest accomplishment. How much more
inexplicable, then, to find out when I myself was in my thirties that perhaps he had not died in a freak accident but had killed himself. How could
he have done this? What could he have been thinking? Was he depressed,
ill, was there some dark secret or financial scandal? Was it something I did?
(This last suspicion was very strong and very primitive, a reflection of the
magical thinking of an eighteen-month-old.) The consensus among most
of the friends and family I have spoken with is that it was probably not an
accident, and that he was probably depressed, but there are still puzzling
inconsistencies in the story. I still do not have definitive answers to all these
questions, and probably never will, but I have now at least been able to embrace and start to work through the pain and uncertainty, instead of simply accepting the family fiction that he had died accidentally—or worse,
that in some way he had never existed.

I would still like to know, though, how he looked at me, what he said,
what he was thinking, when he kissed me goodbye on that last day in October, more than forty years ago. Whenever I leave on a work-related trip,

I hold my girls a little longer, a little tighter than usual, making sure I tell them I love them and will always be with them, no matter where I am. What did my father tell me on that last day, as he picked me up from my crib, as he laid me back down? What could he possibly have said, how could he have found the words to tell me he was leaving? Never having said goodbye to him, I can't imagine how he said goodbye to me.

As a child, whenever I asked, which was not very often, I was told that he had died in a fall from a window, that he had had poor balance, and that this was a terrible accident. I suppose that this seemed so bizarre that maybe I believed it was true; or else, given the way people's expressions and tones of voice would change whenever I brought it up, I got the message that this was not something that was acceptable to discuss. My mother would use an awkward, slightly disapproving tone when she used the phrase "your father," which was the only way that I have ever heard her refer to him. There were no pictures of him anywhere in the house, no letters, no mementos, only the rarest mention of "your father" in conversation—certainly nothing to remind me or preserve the memory of this irreplaceable part of my life. No wonder I had been drawn so unflinchingly to the AIDS epidemic, a gaping black hole of loss that mirrored my own.

It is too easy to find fault with all the ways in which my mother did not help me acknowledge and work through my grief over his death. It is too easy to blame her for not keeping his memory alive. Most importantly, and profoundly, she did what she had to do: she stayed, and she survived. To her credit, in ways that I appreciate more than ever as I experience first-hand the challenges of parenthood, my mother did not let what must have been her own deep rage tarnish any of her feelings toward me. She did not allow the weight of her abandonment by my father to interfere with her attempts to be the best single parent that she could be. If anything, I wish somehow that she could have let me share in some of the pain rather than trying to shield me from it. Perhaps each of us might have felt less alone as we groped our way through the years that followed. Indeed, it was as if we walked side by side in silence under a lingering shadow, a cloud that was all the more ominous because it could not be named.

I will always be grateful for two occasions in my childhood of which I have vivid memories, two times when my mother did *not* try to smooth over or wish away my emotions about my father. Once was when I was in kindergarten and was happily drawing pictures with one of my classmates: we both made colorful crayon drawings depicting my father falling off a building onto the ground. My horrified kindergarten teacher immediately grabbed the pictures and told me that this was very bad, and that I should draw pictures of something happy. When I told my mother what had happened, she came to school and confronted the teacher and told her that I could draw pictures of anything that I liked. The other time was once when I was six and was suddenly filled with an intense desire to see my father. I remember jumping up and down on my bed, screaming, "I want him back, I want him back," and my mother, wisely, just let me continue until I was finished, and then hugged me without saying a word. (Maybe this expression of unconditional love served me as an unconscious example years later in my response to Betty's tirade.)

What has made my father's absence seem more painful, larger than it might have been otherwise, is the fact that I did not even know him long enough to have any conscious memories of him. I felt robbed of this past, not only by my surviving family, who seemed to want to suppress it, but also by him for leaving so soon. When I was growing up, I had few mementos or artifacts from which to construct any memories: a few faded, worn photographs, a couple of his books with his signature on the inside front cover (one the collected plays of Shakespeare, the other essays by Voltaire), an old Gillette razor that my mother said had belonged to him, and little else.

After all these issues and all this hidden history resurfaced for me in my thirties, I asked my mother for any other pictures or personal effects that she may have had. She was able to produce only a few more old photos, but with them she found a few items that had been stored away in a shoe box on top of the closet: his wallet (containing a driver's license, a W-2 tax slip, and a Selective Service card from 1943), his wedding ring, and a pair of wire-rimmed glasses in a faded leather case. I realized that these must have been some of the items found on his body when he died, because the ring had a police identification tag attached to it. I immediately tried on the glasses—they fit my face but were hopelessly blurry—and the ring, which fit my finger perfectly. I put the wallet in my pocket, and walked around the house a little, wondering if I would feel anything special, but nothing much happened. I still have these few items in a wooden box at home, and I am thankful to have some small tokens of remembrance. But mostly, if I stop to think about it, I feel cheated and sad, like I deserved to have more of him.

I have mentioned that I felt a little envious of my dying patients' children whose parents left videotapes or other conscious legacies for them. I am sometimes amazed by the way in which videotape allows us to capture moments in time in a way that was never before possible. When I was growing up, and until not that long ago, there was only the clumsy medium of "home movies," in which, for brief seconds, one could see smiling figures walking mechanically and waving to the camera, speaking without sound, their images projected flickering on the wall and accompanied by the scratchy humming of the projector. Setting up the projector, threading the tape, seeing the 5-4-3-2-1-countdown pattern on the screen before the images appeared—these were all parts of a ritual that also had the effect of making the events preserved seem that much more distant and bygone.

How effortless, by contrast, the way that we now, without thinking twice, pop a tape in the camcorder, record even the most mundane moments of our lives, and instantly play them back on the VCR in a precise rendition of the scene that has just occurred. There is something a little unsettling to me about this, the way in which the past becomes so instantly accessible.

When I was a child, we considered the past as being left behind, not as something capable of being fully and immediately preserved in present time. Like an episode of *Star Trek* in which members of a dying race left a videolike message for future space travelers who might chance across their planet, what is there now to keep us from recording videotaped welcomes to our great-great-grandchildren, in which our voices and images will be as immediate as if they were standing next to us? ("Hello, I have been dead for fifty years, but I thought you might like to know that I was your great-great-grandfather. Have a nice day. . . . ")

Not surprisingly, I do not even have any home movie clips of my father, let alone any videos. I will never hear his voice or see what he looked like when he moved. I feel, again, a little cheated, but in other ways, I am not sorry. I have thought that having a video in which I could see and hear him, with that same immediacy that we now take for granted, might make me feel the loss even more deeply, or might make his decision to kill himself seem all the more unfathomable. Seeing him talking, laughing, playing with me as a baby on a family videotape—these images, I suspect, might make the finality of his death and the mystery of his choice to die seem that much more difficult to accept. So my memories, such as they are, must exist entirely in imagination, which perhaps is not such a bad thing after all.

What finally enabled me to go through the process of reclaiming my past and going beyond it was a combination of the insight that I received through working with my patients and the inner work that I did to confront my own unresolved grief and mourning. To help with the latter, I was fortunate enough to attend a workshop conducted by the staff of the Elisabeth Kübler-Ross Center in April 1989.

I had known of Elisabeth's writing and teaching since early in medical school, when I heard her give a talk on death and dying. In fact, on the day I heard her lecture, as I sat in the back of a huge amphitheater and strained to see this little speck of a person behind the podium up front, I had my first glimpse as an adult of my unresolved grief over my father's death. She answered a question from the audience about suicide, saying that people who kill themselves are still surrounded by love at the moment of death: suddenly, without knowing why, I felt as if something had been unlocked inside of me, and I began to cry, loudly and inconsolably, for a full half hour. The waves of sadness just kept coming over me; it felt as if I was crying from a place I'd never cried from before. Fortunately, Nancy was with me, and she just let me continue crying until it finally stopped, until I turned to her, blinking through the tears, and said, again without knowing why, "I wanted to go with him." After the lecture, I made my way down to the front of the amphitheater, to try to tell Elisabeth about what had happened: she took one look at me, tear-stained cheeks, red eyes, and said, pointing her finger at me, her Swiss accent thick, "You should come to one of my *voorkshops!*" I thanked her, we left the amphitheater, and I spent the rest of the day in an altered state: crying spontaneously, feeling my father's presence in strange ways, imagining myself as a little boy, remembering things I never knew I had forgotten.

It took ten more years before I finally managed to get to one of Elisabeth's workshops. Like a screen that had parted to reveal a clear, bright light and then quickly closed over it again, my well-established defenses kept me blocked off from these powerful feelings and memories until they erupted again that day in the cathedral in 1987. A few months later, I heard about the Elisabeth Kübler-Ross Center in Virginia and became aware of the workshops that the center conducted for people with life-threatening illnesses and their caregivers. These weeklong retreats, called, "Life, Death, and Transition" workshops, were organized using a standard format and were described in the center's brochure as five-day, intense, experiential workshops, intended to help people deal with their unfinished business.

After going to a couple of one-day workshops, run by the center's staff members, and after more than two years of rationalizations and excuses as to why it wasn't yet the right time, I finally signed up to attend one of the five-day workshops in the spring of 1989. I also enrolled with the thought that I should do this because I might learn something that could help me become a better care provider for my patients. But I realized almost immediately, upon arriving at the workshop—which was held at a religious retreat center in Rockland County, outside of New York—that this had nothing to do with my patients and everything to do with me.

It is not my intention here to describe the workshop process in detail. Elisabeth's own well-illustrated book, *Working It Through* (1987), gives a thoughtful and accurate description of one of the Center's workshops. I will, however—without violating the workshops' spirit of confidentiality—describe some of my own experiences with them.

Attending that first workshop and doing this work felt very much like coming home after being away for a long time. I drove up the New York State Thruway, over the Tappan Zee Bridge and into Rockland County, on a beautiful April morning. I was filled with anxiety, uncertainty about what would happen at the workshop, and also a great sense of relief and hopefulness about being there.

As the group assembled to start the workshop, the staff members who were conducting it made clear that everyone was there to do what they needed to do, to access their pain, unresolved grief, or other emotional unfinished business. They also stressed that the workshop environment was a place of absolute safety, unconditional love, and nonjudgment. A combination of teaching, group exercises, and a powerful technique of "externalization" helped participants to release unexpressed emotions—fear, sadness, rage, guilt, love—and to become unburdened in the process. This workshop, and subsequent ones that I attended, left me with the physical sensation that I had learned to breathe again. From my first exposure to this process, and through all my later experiences with it—first by attending additional workshops, then by joining the center's training program, and eventually by being made a staff member, until the center closed in 1995—I continued to be humbled and overwhelmed by the truth, power, safety, and healing that defined this work.

Through the process of group sharing, protected by complete confidentiality and acceptance, people who had never met before—and who knew each other by only their first names—often felt closer to their co-participants by the end of the workshops than they had ever felt to anyone before in their lives. Through this work, I became more aware not only of my own pain and history but also of the profound commonality of experience, needs, and aspirations shared by everyone. The circumstances and the details differ, but all of us, once you scratch the surface, have a history of loss, unresolved grief or anger, family secrets, or other unresolved feelings that stand in the way of our being truly present and unburdened.

The workshop process does not magically remove all of these impediments to "being here now," as the spiritual leader Ram Dass says: rather, it forms the basis of a transformation in outlook and awareness, which then must be integrated back into one's daily life. The workshop facilitators were always quick to stress that this work does not replace psychotherapy or other personal growth work, it merely complements it; yet for some people—and this was my experience—the workshop process can enable them to cross a threshold of understanding and release that they have been unable to reach before.

My first workshop in 1989 took place, appropriately enough, during the week of my thirty-fifth birthday, which made me the same age as my father when he died. In this workshop and in the ones that followed, using simple techniques of externalization and always in the watchful, loving presence of a facilitator, I was able for the first time to experience consciously the loss of my father: the feeling of desertion and abandonment that I had had as an infant and child; the guilt, which in my magical, childlike thinking resulted from the fear that I had caused his death myself; the rage over his having left me; the sadness that I would never be able to see him again or show him what I had accomplished in my life; the disappointment that I would never be able to make him be proud of me; and finally, the empathy and love that I realized I still had for him, the acceptance of what he did, and the hope that his pain had been eased.

Sitting on a mattress, the facilitator seated on one side and the group watching at a respectful distance on the other, I learned to go inside and recall all of the feelings of pain and loss, which were as fresh and as raw as the day that I must have felt them for the first time. Using a rubber hose and telephone books (to express anger, by beating on the phone books), a pillow (to hold), and a towel (to anchor me to the facilitator if I needed to feel safe), I experienced the surfacing and release of a lifetime of pent-up and unexpressed emotions. Sometimes I would talk to my father, sometimes I would talk to the little boy who was abandoned, sometimes to my mother, or to my own children, as I expressed these feelings and said the words that had never been said. Sometimes I thought the tears would never stop. I would finish a piece of emotional work—or think that I had finished it—only to have it well up again inside me when I heard another participant dealing with his or her own loss.

That was the beauty of this work, that in a setting of safety and love, we could all—a group of perfect strangers—come to understand and unburden ourselves of our own pain, while realizing how connected we were by our shared human experience, despite how isolated and alone we might have felt previously. I can say without exaggeration or pretense that these workshops were the single most important and transforming experiences of my life. It is hard to imagine how I could have continued to be fully alive without going through this process.

I came to realize that in certain ways, my work as a physician had been occupying too much of my time; my obsessive need to rescue my unrescuable patients, as well as the ever-increasing demands of our research program, had taken me further and further away from my family and my children. I finally realized, in shock, that I was beginning to abandon my own children, in a different way but with potentially the same effect as my father's more dramatic and violent abandonment of me. I suddenly appreciated that my dizzying work and travel schedule amounted to a choice *not* to be at home. I saw that, in spite of my convincing rationalizations my immersion in work had become a means of maintaining a safe, intellectual distance from Nancy and the girls, prompted by the unconscious fear that anything I loved so much could be abruptly taken away from me and that I would be helpless to prevent the loss. I gave thanks to the universe that I was able to recognize how my work had become a form of running away, compounded by my lack of awareness of my own emotional needs and a fear of being vulnerable to the people that I loved. I gave thanks that I was able to stop this process before it became any more destructive to myself or those around me. These workshops gave me the tools to help make that journey back.

I once asked Elisabeth whether I was doing something wrong, because I kept coming back to the workshops, thinking that I had finished my grieving, but still seemed always to have more tears to shed over my father. She laughed and said that sometimes it seems as though it will never stop, but eventually it does. She said simply that I needed to cry buckets more of tears, and that the loss experienced by a young child whose parent commits suicide is one of the greatest there is. She compared it to the feelings of parents whose own children are murdered. She also predicted that eventually the pain—which then seemed like it took up my whole being—would shrink down to a size where it was always still there but did not dominate my life.

I was actually relieved to hear her say that the pain never went away, for I had realized that in some ways, to give it up entirely might feel like a further loss of my father or his memory. In a way that I have witnessed since then in many of my patients' families, part of me was holding onto the pain of his death because that was all I had left of him. I understood finally that, in fact, not only does the pain not go completely away, but once it is worked through, it forms a scar that can itself be a source of support and healing to oneself and others. In fact, the scar, which is itself the result of an injury, becomes a source of strength.

I realized that this scar was a window for me into the pain of all my patients and was something that deeply connected me to them: a source of empathy, caring, mutuality, and love. I discovered that going through the pain, through the terror—similar to what the poet Robert Bly describes as going through the "wound"—was the only way to get to the other side of it, the only way to begin the process of healing. In effect, I had to go into that black hole—which had remained like something dead and closed off inside me that I carried, unknowingly, my whole life—before I could unburden myself of it, and begin to open my heart to love.

The workshop process also helped me deal with certain current problems in my life that at first I had not even related to my previous history. In my early thirties, not long after becoming a parent, I had begun to experience panic attacks, particularly fears of falling and of being in closed spaces. I had never experienced this before, and it began to be a nuisance at work—sitting in meetings, for example—and especially while traveling. On several occasions I had severe panic attacks while flying in an airplane. The feelings that accompanied these attacks, which lasted a few minutes but seemed like an eternity, were of being suffocated, being out of control, fearing that my heart would suddenly stop beating. Sometimes I saw myself plummeting to the earth from a great height. The connection between these symptoms and my unresolved issues about my father's death came to me in a flash during a workshop. It suddenly occurred to me that these symptoms were a very concrete expression—fears of falling, of suddenly losing control—of all the preconscious fears that I still harbored about his death and the circumstances in which he had died.

Soon after having this realization, I stopped having such severe panic attacks, and whenever I had a premonition or glimmer of one, I was able to prevent it from taking hold by focusing on this insight and talking myself back into reality. Finally, after a few months, I stopped having them altogether.

At the workshop where I first made this connection, I ended my work on the mattress with a vision of myself as a small boy riding on the back of an eagle. Through the tears still in my eyes, I envisioned a red-haired little boy flying freely and without fear, holding securely onto the eagle's back, and I realized that I did not have to be afraid of falling anymore. One of my dear friends, who was one of the other facilitators at that workshop, later made me an oil painting on a small round leather hide, depicting a little boy on the back of an eagle, in the middle of a blue sky, inscribed, "To Peter, who remembers how to fly with the eagle." It still hangs on the wall above my bed.

At the last workshop that I attended as a participant, I realized that there was one more piece of work that I needed to do. One of the facilitators had told me at a previous workshop that for a toddler, the process of developmental separation from the parent is not yet complete, and that part of me may have felt not only that I was responsible for my father's death but that in fact I had died with him—or, as I had blurted out to Nancy after hearing Elisabeth's lecture years before, that I had *wanted* to go with him. (The image of Milagros and her doomed baby again comes to mind.) Indeed, I had become aware of a part of me that felt dead inside, a dead weight that I only fully appreciated when I was able to let it go. Through the externalization process, I was able to go back to the feelings of the eighteen-month-old and separate myself from my father as I imagined the moment of his death. I pictured myself crying out as I ran down the hall after him— even though, of course, I had not been there—and then stopping in front of the open window, only to peer out and see his body crumpled on the roof below. This may seem like bizarre psychodrama, but in fact it was the simple reenactment of this scenario that enabled me to come back into my body and realize that in fact I had not died. I was able to say goodbye to him in a way that I had not been able to before and was able to reclaim that part of myself from the realm of the dead. I was also able to understand for the first time that his choice to die—if that's what it was—had nothing to do with me, and came from a totally different place than his love for me, which did not die.

This reenactment was matched only by the physical experience, years later, of visiting the site where he had died and going through the psychic process again. I left that workshop feeling as if I had shed an old skin, and that my new skin fit a little more snugly, comfortably. I felt truly able to go on with my life, simply put, for the first time that I could remember.

I also understood then, with a kind of wistfulness, that, irrevocably, my life, my choices, and the person that I had become were all inseparable from the fact that my father *had* died. What direction would I have taken, what would my sensibilities and yearnings be if he had *lived?* This was difficult to comprehend. What would it have been like to have his presence in my life, not only as a loving father but also as someone whom I would have had to separate from, fight with, surpass? What would my feelings for him be if he were not a mythical and mysterious figure who had been violently taken from me but rather someone whom I knew in all the monotonous familiarity of daily life? What would it have been like if I had not remained an only child? What would adolescence have been like, to have had a male authority figure telling me to cut my hair, to turn down the volume as I sat in my room lined with wall-to-wall psychedelic Day-Glo posters, stereo speakers blaring Jimi Hendrix or the Doors? The scenarios were endless.

Finally, how would I have learned about pain, loss, and healing, if he had lived? I am certain that I would have eventually learned these lessons, but now I see that I owe much of my own growth and self-knowledge to the process of coming to terms with his death. In a strange but unavoidable way, my life—including much that was good with my life—is inseparably connected with his death.

My personal journey through my own history and back again was prompted, in part, by the countless small ways in which my work experience as a physician in the AIDS epidemic kept bringing me back to the central, unresolved issue in my life. It may be fitting, then, that the process of becoming aware of my past was ultimately beneficial not only in my life but also to my work. Once I became aware that I had never come to terms with the loss of my father, I began the work of grieving both for my father, which I had never done, and for all of my patients who had died. After going through this process, I found that I had become better able to be with my patients in their pain, to support them without feeling the blind compulsion to rescue them from something from which they could not be rescued, and to accompany them as they approached death without feeling that I had somehow betrayed their trust.

I have learned that the greatest gift that I can give to patients is to allow the awareness of my own pain and loss to deepen my solidarity with them, as they stand facing their illness and death. Working through my own pain has been the key to enabling me to accompany other people through theirs. With every loss we experience, and every struggle we survive, our lives become that much richer a source for empathy and connection with other people, as we all make our way along the human trail of living in the world. Recognizing death, accepting it, grieving our losses—these are the prerequisites of truly being able to be present with people who are facing life-threatening illness. Acknowledging and experiencing the pain allows the heart to open, enabling us to experience joy in a way that otherwise would not be possible.

This, of course, is one of the central riddles of human existence—that life is finite, while our dreams are not, or that, as has been said, we are all born and die in the middle of history—and such have been the themes of tragic drama and literature for centuries. What I learned through personal experience, however, which I could never have learned in a lifetime of reading or seminars, was that it is only by embracing this paradox and walking through the dark side that you can truly become aware of the light. Ten years ago I would have dismissed this imagery as airheaded, New Age nonsense: now I know it to be a basic and powerful truth.

I hesitate to compare my own history with the challenges of people living with AIDS. Nevertheless, a similarity strikes me in the way that some of my patients have come to view AIDS as a gift, as a blessing in disguise. AIDS is nothing that they would ever wish on themselves or anyone else, but once they have confronted and dealt with it, the disease has enabled them to embrace living in ways that they had never been able to do before. Likewise, although I would trade it in an instant for a father to have grown up with, I now see that the experience of my father's suicide has become an integral part of who I am, and a source for clarity, empathy, insight, and strength. We are all wounded by the world: the key is to recognize our wounds, nurse them, and go beyond them as we are healed, wearing our scars quietly like discreet badges of honor. I am now convinced that the physician's fear of death, and his or her own unexpressed grief, are the biggest impediments to true empathy, and result instead in pity, despair, revulsion, and the kind of numbing detachment that finds refuge in technological interventions and a narrow medical model of care.

I do not wish to indulge in the romanticization of death, nor in the tragic imagery of the nobility of dying young. I cannot sit and listen to a young father with AIDS, as he bargains with God to be allowed to live long enough to dance with his eight-year-old daughter at her wedding, without feeling the crushing sense of injustice that this disease inspires. Indeed, it has been very gratifying to me, and a great relief as a clinician, to experience the dramatic advances in the medical care of people with AIDS over the past decade. These advances have affected the clinical course of HIV infection in profound ways and have helped to convert a rapidly fatal illness into a more chronic and treatable, albeit incurable, disease.

Nevertheless, I can recall the simple and immediate nature of my relationships with patients at an earlier time in the AIDS epidemic. Before our current therapies existed, we coexisted with patients in the grim but complete knowledge that all that physicians could do was to be there, to bear witness, to support, to comfort, and to accompany patients through their illness. What enabled, or even entitled, us to do this was simply our commitment not to abandon the patient and our experience in having traveled this road with others before. I believe that this fundamental connectedness with the patient best characterizes the history of the physician-patient relationship over the centuries, until powerful forces over the past several decades have fragmented and distorted it, often in the name of specialization, expertise, or increasing technical sophistication.

At times it has been ironic to observe how the rapid introduction of medical interventions for AIDS—which, thankfully, have increased in number and complexity in recent years—has resulted in some ways in the tendency to overmedicalize the disease and lose sight of the important fundamental dynamics of life and death that still, ultimately, define it.

Paradoxically, the *lack* of treatment options for HIV in the early years of the epidemic brought with it an important awareness of the shared humanity between patient and care provider. Some of this awareness, and the humility and solidarity that accompanied it, are at risk of being lost in the technical maze of what has become HIV medical care.

It is particularly important to maintain this awareness, as the epidemic shifts into more and more disenfranchised populations, both in this country and worldwide. It is estimated that by the year 2000, more than 90 percent of the world's forty million AIDS cases will be in developing countries, and the majority of United States cases will involve injection drug users, women, and their sexual partners, increasingly concentrated in poor populations of color. These developments will result in a growing chasm between the medical-technical interventions to treat HIV infection and the vast numbers of people who might benefit from them.

The challenge is that we not let our rapidly emerging medical model distract us from what may be more pressing—if seemingly intractable— issues in our patients' lives. It becomes more expedient to write a stack of prescriptions from the burgeoning pharmacopoeia of HIV therapeutics than to stop to think about the profound isolation, marginalization, and threats to survival that many of our patients must confront on a daily basis. We must not let the eagerly awaited advent of the therapeutic era for AIDS have as an unintended consequence the loss of empathy and the doctor's willingness not only to treat, but simply to *be* with, the patient.

It has always seemed ironic to me how those who are confronted with dying are much more aware of living, and, in some cases, are able to live in a much more immediate and intense way than those whose daily lives are dulled by the unconscious assumption that time is unlimited. Many patients have told me that having AIDS has allowed and required them to dispense with all of the superficial distractions and wasted energy that take up so much of our attention, and has led them to focus on what was truly important in their lives. As Javon once said to me, "AIDS is kind of like life, just speeded up," which describes well the accelerated process in which, over a period of weeks to months, people with AIDS may have to confront issues in the life cycle that normally would have taken years to decades: the death of peers and family, the loss of sexual and other physical functions, deterioration in cognition and memory, and the effects of aging on one's bodily appearance. Martin once remarked to me with a little bitterness, but also some satisfaction, that AIDS had taught him who his friends really were. And I remember the further example of Javon, for whom confronting death had enabled him to undergo a spiritual conversion, stop using drugs, and reconcile with his family—as he had said, in effect, he had to die in order to learn how to live.

Ultimately, for both patients and physicians, AIDS is about letting go. It is only through a process of letting go of fear and blame, then accepting our own vulnerability and powerlessness, that we can become truly powerful. This is the central wisdom of all the twelve-step recovery programs, in which the recognition of one's powerlessness in the face of the addiction is the first step in being able to overcome it. It is only by letting go that we can, as the great labor organizer Mother Jones put it, "Mourn the dead and fight like hell for the living," that we can get on with the process of living and dying that all of us have to confront, beyond the artificial distinctions between physician and patient.

I often recall my last conversation with a patient in her early thirties whom I will call Maria. She had been ill with AIDS for several years and seemed to be lingering on well past the point that anyone thought she would survive. She had a six-year-old daughter, whom I will call Lisa, who was being cared for by her aunt because Maria was already too weak to care for her. The aunt had agreed to raise the child after Maria's death; this had helped to relieve Maria's concerns, but it made her feel guilty that she was leaving her only child.

In fact, it became clear that this was the only reason that she had survived as long as she had. She felt that she needed to die but couldn't. She was also saddened because Lisa at times was angry with her for not being able to play with her and not being there to put her to bed at night. Finally, when I asked her what she was most afraid of, she said she was afraid that by dying she would be betraying her little girl, that this would somehow be a sign to the child that she didn't truly love her. After we talked about it, she came to realize that these two things were totally separate, that she had to die but that nothing could ever take away the bond between her and her daughter. I encouraged her to talk to Lisa about this, and to let her know that she would always love her and always be with her in her heart, no matter what happened. The next day she spent the whole day with her child, saying everything that she needed to say. Two days later, she died, peacefully, at home.

And for me, the then-thirty-nine-year-old physician, with the eighteen-month-old boy inside who had never had that last conversation with his father, nothing could have been more gratifying.

## 4  Reconstruction

On the fortieth anniversary of my father's death, October 17, 1995, I went
to visit the building in lower Manhattan from which he had fallen (or,
more likely, jumped) to his death. From the moment I began to reclaim the
history of my father's death, I knew that I would one day need to go to
the place where he had died. I realized that I needed to do this to complete
the circle, to help put closure on this event, which had occasioned so much
emotional work.

I had asked my mother several times for information about the specific
place and time of his death, but she had not been able to find the relevant
documents. During the six months leading up to this anniversary, I had
also searched, in vain, through virtual stacks of old New York newspa-

pers, on microfilm in the basement of Yale's Sterling Library, looking for some clue, some missing piece of the puzzle that could shed light on these long-hidden secrets. Sitting in front of the large microfilm screen, I went through a succession of small, dusty cardboard boxes, each containing a thick spool. I became adept at threading these reels onto the machine, one after another, carefully scanning page after page of the *New York Times,* the *Herald Tribune,* and the *World Telegram and Sun* from the week of October 17, 1955.

From my microfilm searches, I could report at length about the weather that week (a severe storm with widespread flooding had affected much of the northeast); what football teams and race horses had won over the weekend ("Giants Down Cardinals in Home Opener," "Michigan State Beats Notre Dame, 21–7, Army Loses, Yale, Navy, Harvard Win," "Nashua Takes Gold Cup"); what was playing on Broadway (Julie Harris in *The Lark,* Van Heflin in *A View from the Bridge,* Shelley Winters and Ben Gazzara in previews for *A Hatful of Rain*); and what was in the movie theaters (*Cinerama Holiday, Mister Roberts,* and *The Trouble with Harry,*— the latter "introducing Shirley McLaine").

I even studied the television listings for the evening of October 17 to see which programs he had never returned home to see—although, from what little I had learned about him, I didn't think he was much inclined to watch television—*Burns and Allen, The Liberace Show, Godfrey's Talent Scouts,* and *I Love Lucy.*

I carefully reviewed what was on the front pages the day after he died:

*Wilson Sees Cost of Arms Leveling; Meets Eisenhower*
*Nixon Optimistic on Big 4 Parley*
*Johnson Seeking Coalition to Give South Key to '56*
*Floods Receding, President Speeds Help for 3 States*

Scanning these headlines, and then reading every page of that day's newspapers, line by line, I searched in vain for any mention of my father's death. I repeated this process with the next day's newspapers, and the next.

Still I found nothing. I felt puzzled, sitting at the microfilm scanner, wondering why an event that was of such great importance to me seemed to have gone unnoticed by the rest of the world.

All that I could find about him was a small notice in the obituary section of the *Times* on October 19:

> SELWYN—Aaron, suddenly Oct. 17, 1955, beloved husband of Amy,
> dear father of Peter, devoted son and brother. Services private.
> Wednesday, 11:30 A.M., Riverside Memorial Chapel, 1 Ocean Parkway,
> Brooklyn.

Still, the specifics eluded me.

Finally, a little less than a month before the fortieth anniversary date, my mother produced a yellowed, onionskin document, a memo, several pages long, dictated by the attorney who had handled my father's estate and the investigation of the circumstances of his death. The memo described, in unemotional detail, the events of his last day:

He went to work that morning as if nothing were out of the ordinary, according to the report, and spent the morning at his job as an accountant for an auto dealership in Queens. He left the office at 1 P.M., having mentioned to one of his coworkers who was later interviewed that he was going to buy a snowsuit for his son, Peter.

Then, with no explanation of his whereabouts in the interim, he was last seen alive by a cleaning woman between 6:30 and 7:00 P.M. on the twenty-third floor of a building at 30 Broad Street in the financial district of lower Manhattan. This was a building in which he reportedly had once had some business dealings, but he had no explicable reason to be there on that day. The cleaning woman reported that he had asked her once and then again a second time for the key to the men's room (which had no window).

The report then states that sometime after 7 P.M. but before 7:20, his body was found on the roof of the adjacent, lower building, 40 Broad

Street. (How considerate, I thought, not to do this on the street side, with all the pedestrians and traffic.) A pair of his wire-rimmed eyeglasses was found on the window sill of an open office window on the twenty-third floor of 30 Broad, overlooking the building next door. I remembered, reading this, that my mother had once told me that he had uncharacteristically left his gold watch—which was specifically designated in his will to be left for me—at home on the day that he died. A business card was allegedly found in his pocket, which was reported to have written on it, "Cremation, no mourners." I shuddered as I read this: after so many years of elusiveness and mystery, this document had a chilling matter-of-factness.

Not knowing what I would find, but knowing that I needed to finish what I had begun, I decided to visit this site in Manhattan on the upcoming anniversary of his death. On the afternoon of October 17, 1995, I reluctantly took the train from New Haven into Grand Central Station. Taking the subway downtown, I soon found myself facing 30 Broad Street, one of the older buildings on the street, with yellow bricks, decorative cornices, and a series of terraced upper floors. I made a mental count up to what I thought was the twenty-third floor, and—probably looking on the outside like another wide-eyed tourist who had come to New York to bring home a souvenir of the Big Apple—I took several photos of the building. The building at 40 Broad Street, in contrast, looked like it had been built recently, with more contemporary architectural lines, and I noticed also that the roof of the new building at 40 Broad was only a couple of stories lower than the twenty-third floor of 30 Broad. After careful inspection, I could detect the old, faded roofline against the side of 30 Broad from what must have been the top of the building formerly standing next to it, which had been only ten or twelve stories tall. More than enough distance for a fatal fall, I thought.

I gathered my backpack and my composure and walked into the lobby of 30 Broad. I was immediately stopped by the West Indian security guard, who asked me what office I was going to. Realizing how silly I must sound as I heard myself talking, I said, "I am not going to a particular office; I need to check something on the twenty-third floor." After making me repeat myself several times to make sure he had heard correctly, he raised an eyebrow and said, "What do you mean, you need to *check* something?"

"Well, I need to visit a certain office." Clearly making a mental assessment to see what type of lunatic I was, he gruffly directed me to the brokerage firm that had a storefront office on the side of the building. The firm, he said, was the sole occupant of the twenty-third floor. "You better go talk to them, maybe *they* can help you."

I dutifully walked outside and around the corner, and entered the office of busy young stock traders—well-fed, white shirts a little rumpled by that hour of the late afternoon, suit jackets off, suspenders—where one of the clerks soon came over and asked if he could help me. "I hope so," I said, "you see, I have what will sound like a very strange request." I proceeded to tell him, calmly, that my father had died forty years ago to that day in a fall from a twenty-third floor office of 30 Broad, and I wanted to go upstairs to visit the scene of this event.

He smiled nervously, shifting his weight from one foot to the other. "Wait here," he blurted out, and went to a back office to confer with his boss. One of the office vice presidents quickly emerged, also eyeing me suspiciously, and first directed me to speak with the building manager. I explained the circumstances to him, and showed him the attorney's report documenting the events of that day. Again, he hesitated nervously, referring me once more to the building manager. When I asked finally whether would it be such an intrusion for me to go up and look for five minutes, he looked me over again, sizing me up. Then, in a defining moment that seemed to last forever, I saw his expression change. His face softened, and he grabbed his jacket. He turned to the group of brokers standing around, declared, "I'm outta here," and then turned to me and said, "Come on, I'll take you up myself."

We walked back through the lobby of 30 Broad, past the watchful raised eye of the security guard. I showed my guide the attorney's memo again as we rode up in the elevator, and I felt my heart pounding as we got closer to the twenty-third floor. As we walked off the elevator, I was at first taken aback to see that the whole floor was one bright, well-lit, contemporary brokerage office suite, circa 1995. I was startled to see that it was not the dark brown 1950s corridor with rows of adjacent, separate offices— frosted glass doors with hand-painted lettering, wooden door frames, marble-tiled floors, and globe lamps hanging down in the hall—that I had envisioned. My newfound friend quickly led me through the sprawling, open office suite to the corner office that had two windows overlooking 40 Broad Street. He opened the door without knocking—saying to two young brokers who were working at a large table, "Go on, you guys, make yourselves scarce; I need to take care of some business for five minutes"— and ushered me into the room as the men quickly gathered up their papers and left.

I went over to the window sill, ran my fingers along the edge, and peered out and down at the top of the new adjacent building, imagining where the roof of the old 40 Broad building had stopped, a good distance down. I looked out the window and tried to imagine my father's last moments here, trying to visualize his trajectory as he hurtled to the roof below—thinking as I did so how much this exercise was like my attempts had been as a kindergartner to come to terms with what had happened by drawing a picture of it. I found myself posing very basic questions, none of which would ever be answered. Did he lose consciousness before he hit? Did he feel the impact? Were his bones crushed by the fall? Did he bounce, or just collapse in a lifeless heap? Was there blood? What was he thinking as he fell?

I recalled a conversation I once had had with my older daughter, when she was about six. We were driving in Manhattan, nowhere near the financial district, when she asked me, spontaneously, whether the building we were passing was the one my father had fallen from. Then she had said, also unprompted, "I'm sure he was thinking while he was falling, 'I love my little boy very much.'" (Both girls have known since they were small that my father died by falling from a building, and now they know that it was probably a suicide—I have vowed not to make the same mistakes of secrecy over again.)

As I stood there looking out the window, surveying the scene, I telescoped years of mystery and uncertainty into five minutes. It all seemed so ordinary, so mundane, not the stage for such high ancestral drama. After I had mentally catalogued every inch of landscape that I could see from that window, I turned away and looked at my new friend. He said that he remembered the earlier building at 40 Broad, and that indeed its roof had stopped ten or twelve stories lower down. We walked out, back toward the elevators.

On the way out we went by the bathroom, which he told me had not been changed from its original location when the floor had been renovated into one big open suite. I went inside, remembering that this was where the cleaning woman had last seen my father before he died. The bathroom looked old—indeed it looked as if it probably had the same porcelain toilets and marble stall dividers that had been there on that October day forty years before. I looked in the mirror, wondering whether this was the same mirror where my father had last looked at his reflection, wondering what he saw. I quickly scanned the walls, ceiling, floor, with the fleeting thought that maybe there was a message or a sign somewhere, but of course there was not.

On the way downstairs in the elevator, I thanked my companion again for his kindness, and he asked me offhandedly whether I had any money in the stock market. I told him I had a small amount in a few mutual funds, and then he asked, "What kind of a doctor are you anyway?" I told him I took care of people with AIDS, and he said, "Oh," nodding seriously. After a pause, he then gave me his business card and said, "Listen, if you ever want to talk about some investments, just give me a call." We shook hands, I thanked him again, and I walked out onto Broad Street, feeling suddenly like I could go anywhere, and also like I had no destination.

The air felt fresh and clean, but it was starting to get cold, and the shadows were quickly filling the streets of the financial district. After walking for a while, I circled back to Broad Street, and stopped into a coffee shop that was on the ground level of number 60. I ordered a hot tea and a muffin, and the matronly waitress said, as she served me, "Now drink up, child, you know you're gonna need that hot tea with the weather changing, and don't forget to bundle up when you go outside." I smiled, thanked her, and tried to imagine, as she walked away, whether my father had received any such caring advice as he made the rounds of his last day.

I stepped back out onto the sidewalk, heading toward Wall Street as I joined the swelling tide of rush hour pedestrians. I gave a last look up at number 30 Broad as I walked by, putting my hands in my pockets and raising my jacket collar against the chill. All at once, I felt a powerful urge to go home.

I entered the subway, rode uptown, reached Grand Central Station, found my train, and settled into a window seat, moving mechanically but satisfied, knowing that each step was bringing me closer to home. "I need to go home," I told myself decisively, just as I knew that *he* could not, or did not, on that day. I had a visceral realization then about the finality of his life and death: his life had ended there, on that day, at that time, in that place. He had made his choices and decisions for whatever reasons he had, and there were no more decisions or yearnings or struggles. But my life continued. I took my pulse—strong, steady, persistent—and felt the comforting rattling and shifting of the train.

How many years of my life had I spent not being sure whether or not I had died with him, or else, unconsciously, feeling guilty over having survived. All of the workshops and grief work that I had done had prepared me for that moment. Being able to leave him, symbolically, on the roof of that building meant being able to go on with my life in a way that suddenly needed no explanation, no justification. I smiled as I saw my reflection in the train window, against the dark night outside, feeling content in the company of so many other commuters on their way home.

When I got home, a little after eight, I paused as I stepped out of my car in the driveway and looked from outside the house at the warm lights inside. As I opened the door, I heard the animated voices of my kids. I hugged them tighter than usual that night, savoring their smell, their texture, their sweetness. I felt a pang of wistfulness as I heard them say, "Good night, Daddy, I love you," thinking that I had never had the opportunity to say those words myself. But mostly I felt happy, unburdened, and, like the protagonist of John Berger's book, a fortunate man.

A couple of days later, I was flying back to New York on a shuttle flight after a morning trip to Washington, where I had given a talk at an AIDS meeting. As the plane banked over La Guardia Airport, I looked down at the vast expanses of Queens cemeteries, the tiny stones arrayed in neat, long rows. I remembered that the crematory where my father's ashes were stored was on the edge of one of these cemeteries, though I could not identify it from the air. After we landed, I felt the urge to stop by there on my way home. It was a ten-minute drive from the airport, a route that I had become familiar with after several previous trips.

Several years before, I had gone for the first time to see the place where his ashes were kept (I am still not certain what verb to use to describe the peculiar way that the urns are displayed in the crematorium: buried? stored? housed?) and had found my way to an imposing, yellow brick building. I knew that he had been cremated but had only recently learned where his ashes were. In my thirties, as I became more aware of my father's absence in my life, I decided that I wanted to visit this place.

After I asked my mother—as with the attorney's letter about his death, it took several nudges—she had given me a faded certificate, notarized, from 1955, which was the deed to the "cremains" (a word new to me) of my father. The name and address of the crematorium were on the certificate. There was no telephone number, and when I called directory assistance there was no listing under that name. I looked in the Queens Yellow Pages under crematoria and found one that had the same address as the one on the certificate. I called the number, and the secretary who answered the phone confirmed that the company had indeed changed names but that it was the same site as that indicated on the document.

A few weeks later, I took my New York City atlas and headed off to Queens. Like the Bronx before I came to work there, Queens—though the borough of my birth—seemed to be an undifferentiated expanse, with few landmarks: La Guardia Airport, Shea Stadium, the old World's Fair Grounds. I would have been hopelessly lost there without a map. After several wrong turns, squinting to make out the street names on the atlas, I finally found the crematorium. When I arrived at the small complex of buildings, the first thing I noticed was a large smokestack at the far corner of one of them.

As I noticed several years later, on my visit to the financial district, it felt a little anticlimactic as I walked for the first time up to the entrance door and the office of the crematorium. I told the receptionist that I wanted to see the ashes of my father and gave her his name. She smiled, took out a large ledger, and scrolled down the pages of names with her index finger until she found his. "Yes, here it is," she announced, "number 627, Room of Peace." She asked whether I had ever been there before, and when I said that I hadn't, she buzzed the intercom for one of the funeral directors. A cheerful woman promptly appeared, with short, curly hair and a dark blue suit; she carried a large three-ring binder in one arm.

After introducing herself, she said, pointing to the binder, "I wanted to bring this along because it's hard to find your way around some of the older rooms without a guide." We walked past the Hall of Remembrance, the Room of Serenity, and several other soothing locales, finally reaching the Room of Peace. Passing through the other rooms, I was struck by the floor-to-ceiling display of glass cases. The cases were built into the walls, forming niches that appeared to have a depth of about two feet; the only visible aspect was the glass that formed the front surface of the wall of niches. Some of the larger ones were several feet across and held ornate, porcelain urns, along with photographs, plastic flowers, and other mementos; the smallest ones seemed to be no more than six inches in width and height and reminded me of post office boxes, or stacks of shoe boxes in the back room of a shoe store.

The Room of Peace, tucked away at the end of a corridor, was a small, dimly lit room no more than ten feet wide in both directions. After we turned on an additional light, which was on a timer—like the lights found in library stacks, in the old out-of-the-way sections that are rarely used— I saw that the room's four walls were made up of row upon row of small metal plates, each inscribed simply with a name and two dates. Most of the metal plates were dulled and tarnished, and it was hard to make out the lettering on some of them. I noticed that the latter dates on these little rectangles—these seemed to resemble post office boxes even more than the cases we had passed along the way—were all prior to 1960. It struck me that this was like a forgotten landfill, belonging to another era, left in silence long after the active process of turning bodies to ashes and storing them in little niches had moved on to other rooms in the facility.

My heart started pounding as I scanned the wall of names, realizing that once I saw his I would be given a new kind of proof that he had really existed. I looked for several minutes and couldn't locate his metal plate, and my guide opened her three-ring binder and started flipping through plastic-covered sheets containing diagrams of the different rooms. "Let's see, Selwyn, number 627 . . . here's Feinberg, Glassman, Mendoza—oh, here it is, in the corner right above Berkowitz!" I looked over to the side of the room that corresponded to the diagram in the book, and, peering hard into the shadows to make it out, saw the discolored metal plate in the uppermost corner of the wall that was indeed inscribed with my father's name. As I stood staring up at it, my guide discreetly excused herself, and I was left alone in the small room.

It seemed appropriate, symbolically, that my father's ashes were hidden away here, in the room that time forgot, and that even to find them I had had to be guided by maps through unfamiliar places—first through Queens, then through the facility itself. Seeing his name, though, made it all seem real in a way that it hadn't before. I really *did* have a father, after all; he was more than just a memory that everyone in my family seemed intent on suppressing. At the same time, seeing the neglected pigeonhole where his ashes had been kept untended for all these years—it occurred to me that I was perhaps the first person who had come to visit him in nearly forty years—I felt the urge to bring his remains more into the light. After spending a half hour in the Room of Peace, having an imaginary dialogue with him, I returned through the other rooms and corridors to the main office, where I asked to meet with the head funeral director.

After a few minutes, I was ushered into a wood-paneled office, and shook hands with the president of the crematorium, a boyish-looking man in his thirties whose family had been running the establishment for many years. I explained the circumstances of my visit, and he discussed different options for moving my father's ashes to a more accessible, visible, and well-frequented section of the facility. He took me to see the Hall of Tranquility, which was much more open, well-lit, and had fresh flowers in front of many of the glass cases. I thanked him, and told him that I would discuss this with my mother, who still held the deed to my father's burial site.

Several weeks later, I returned with my mother—she had quickly agreed to make this trip with me, hoping, I think, that this would help put this all to rest for me—and we were shown the newer site. We discussed the different options—$1,500 for the smallest niche, $5,000 for the largest, prices also varying based on height above the floor—and selected a vacant case in one of the upper tiers. The funeral director pointed out a larger case slightly lower on the wall, which was big enough to hold two urns, and asked, somewhat unctuously, whether my mother had considered purchasing a space for herself so that she could be next to him someday. She blurted out "No" with a shudder, as if this were the last thing in the world that would ever occur to her. I gave her credit for agreeing to go through this with me, and resented the funeral director's presumption; he quickly got the message that he shouldn't pursue this any further.

We returned to his office, signed some papers, and, as part of the process, transferred the deed to my father's niche from my mother to me (her suggestion, not mine, but one that I appreciated). A month later, I received a letter at home from the crematorium indicating that the transfer had been effected and also containing the new deed, with the new location specified on it. I looked at this document and had a feeling of quiet satisfaction as I realized that I would always now know his location, his coordinates, like some archaeological site that had been brought to light after years of digging, its artifacts finally unearthed, cleaned, classified, and put on display.

I was thinking of those earlier visits on that day in October 1995, as I drove from La Guardia through Queens, arrived at the building, and parked outside. I walked up to the wrought-iron door and pushed the buzzer to be let in to the Hall of Tranquility. The buzzer sounded and I went down the stairs, into the room with the hundreds of little glass cases, row upon row, that no longer seemed so strange to me. I found his little bronze-colored shoe box, with the shiny plate on the front behind the glass: "Aaron Selwyn, 1920–1955." It was right where I had last left it, in one of the upper rows that had begun to fill in since my last visit the previous year. His niche was up a few rows, still out of reach, and I could touch the glass only by jumping up and tapping it, arm outstretched, for a split second. Notwithstanding the move from the Room of Peace, there was still something inaccessible about it—fitting, I thought, as I looked up at it, unable to touch it.

I stood, looking up at his nameplate, and became aware that, with the passing of time, my relationship to him in the life cycle was also changing. Seeing his birth and death dates, I was at once reminded that I had already outlived him by six years and was beginning to experience some of the bodily changes of middle age that he had not lived long enough to experience. I imagined myself for a moment not as his son but as a dutiful older brother, stopping by to see him and to let him know how I was doing in the world. I envisioned myself being even older—at forty-five, fifty, sixty, even eighty—coming down those same marble steps into this same quiet room, where his memory would always be frozen in the time when the clock suddenly stopped at age thirty-five. Finally, I could see myself as a frail, elderly man of ninety (arbitrary choice, I suppose, but I optimistically picked my grandfather's last decade), making one last visit to see the ashes of the man who by then would be young enough to be my grandson, saying goodbye with all the memories, experiences, joys, and sorrows of a lifetime. That was a satisfying image, and I decided to hold onto it.

Then my mind and its montage of images began to go in another direction: standing in that same spot, I closed my eyes and pictured myself first as an infant, then a toddler, kindergartner, grade-schooler, bar mitzvah boy, adolescent, then in high school, college, medical school, a bridegroom, husband, father, physician, AIDS specialist: all these stages of my life overlapped each other like a stack of snapshots and merged inside me, coexisting across time and space. I felt at that moment, simultaneously, both a sense of connection with my father and completeness in myself—I had come this far, safely and whole, and could go on without feeling like a big piece of me was still missing. As I had learned, the wound doesn't go away, but after healing it forms a scar that can be a source of strength. I could see and feel instinctively how our paths had truly diverged, and I could finally understand and describe the boundaries that defined our separateness and our connection. He was my father. He died. I was his son. I lived.

I survived the fall.

I took one more look up at the box of ashes with the burnished name-plate, nodded, smiled, and walked upstairs and out the door into the bright, afternoon sunlight.